THE
BONDAGE
BREAKER®

DEVOTIONAL

NEIL T. ANDERSON

HARVEST HOUSE PUBLISHERS
EUGENE, OREGON

Cover by Bryce Williamson

THE BONDAGE BREAKER is a registered trademark of The Hawkins Children's LLC. Harvest House Publishers, Inc., is the exclusive licensee of the federally registered trademark THE BONDAGE BREAKER.

The Bondage Breaker® Devotional
Copyright © 2019 by Neil T. Anderson
Published by Harvest House Publishers
Eugene, Oregon 97408
www.harvesthousepublishers.com

ISBN 978-0-7369-7589-6 (pbk)
ISBN 978-0-7369-7590-2 (eBook)

Library of Congress Cataloging-in-Publication Data is on file at the Library of Congress, Washington, DC.

I want to thank Harvest House Publishers for encouraging me to write this devotional, which is a daily encounter with key concepts that govern our lives. It gave me the opportunity to compress the best of what I have learned in 25 years of formal education, 45 years of ministry, and as the author of 70-plus books into 200 short readings. If I had to reduce the content any further, I would simply say, "Love the Lord your God with all your heart and love your neighbor as yourself."

As the founder of Freedom in Christ Ministries, nothing means more to me than passing the mantle of leadership to faithful men and women who will continue the work of setting captives free and healing the wounds of the brokenhearted. With a great deal of love, respect, and gratitude, I dedicate this book to Rich and Shirley Miller, who shepherd the ministry in the United States, and to Steve and Zoe Goss, who direct the work internationally. The ministry has greatly expanded under their leadership, and they have proved themselves to be faithful stewards who are entrusting the message to other faithful men and women. To God be the glory.

Neil T. Anderson

LIFE

Take hold of the eternal life to which you were called.

1 TIMOTHY 6:12 NASB

In the beginning God created the heavens and the earth" (Genesis 1:1 NASB). The Hubble Space Telescope enables us to view the extravagance of creation, and what we see is beyond our ability to comprehend. We can only marvel as we stare into space. "The heavens are telling of the glory of God; and their expanse is declaring the work of His hands" (Psalm 19:1 NASB). The universe has supernovas, galaxies, and stars so large that if depicted on a printed page, they would render the earth a tiny dot in comparison. All of this created matter is finite, devoid of life, and did not originate from pre-existing matter. On the other hand, the Creator is living and infinite, the Mind behind the universe. How big is God?

Earth and possibly other planets have organic life in the form of plants, birds, animals, and fish. Such life is all subject to the natural law of death. It perpetuates its species by sowing seeds or by other means for the next generation before it dies. "Then the LORD God formed man of dust from the ground, and breathed into his nostrils the breath of life; and man became a living being" (Genesis 2:7 NASB). Something new and totally different was introduced into the universe. God shared His divine and eternal life with Adam, who was created in His image and likeness. Adam's soul was in union with God.

My response to God is:

God, keep me in union with you.
You are big and I am small. It's
your breath in my lungs so let me
focus my attention on you and not
my problems. I know you have
a plan for me.

5

WHO AM I?

When I look at your heavens, the work of your fingers, the moon
and the stars, which you have set in place, what is man that you
are mindful of him, and the son of man that you care for him?

PSALM 8:3-4

W"hat is man?" is an ontological question concerning the nature
of "being." Five centuries before Christ, Thales of Miletus was
asked, "What is the most difficult?" He replied, "To know thyself."
Twenty-five centuries later, science is no closer to answering "What is
man?" We know far more about the chemical makeup of the body, but
that tells us nothing about who we are when absent from the body and
present with the Lord. Psychology can describe but cannot unlock the
mystery of the *person*. Being a carpenter, engineer, parent, or Ameri-
can citizen defines only what we do and where we live, not who we are.
Biology is the study of plants and animals, but none bear the image
nor likeness of God. Science cannot answer the most basic of all questions: Who are we, and why are we here?

The only "ology" that can properly explain who we are is theology.
We are children of Almighty God, created in His image and likeness.
Under God's guidance and enabling presence, we are working out our
God-given destiny. "We are his workmanship, created in Christ Jesus
for good works, which God prepared beforehand, that we should walk
in them" (Ephesians 2:10).

My response to God is:

Thank-you that I am your child.
I feel like an orphan in my family
of origin but I am a daughter
of the King of kings
I am a child of God.

DEATH

The wages of sin is death, but the free gift of God
is eternal life in Christ Jesus our Lord.

ROMANS 6:23 NASB

When Adam sinned, he died spiritually. His soul was no longer in union with God. Death means "to be separate from," and life means "to be in union with." Death is the end of a relationship but not existence. Adam remained physically alive because his soul was still in union with his body, but sin had separated him from God. "Just as sin came into the world through one man, and death through sin, and so death spread to all men because all sinned" (Romans 5:12). "And you were dead in the trespasses and sins" (Ephesians 2:1). Every descendent of Adam is born physically alive but spiritually dead.

Before the fall, Adam was accepted, secure, and significant. Who was Adam after the fall? What was his purpose? Adam had no choice but to find his own way in this world, relying on his own strength and natural resources. How could he not feel rejected, insecure, and insignificant? Can we make a name for ourselves and find acceptance, security, and significance by our appearance, performance, and social status? The wise King Solomon tried, and then he concluded that "all is vanity" (Ecclesiastes 1:2 NASB). "The wages of sin is death, but…"

My response to God is:

Jesus' death showed God's love
Jesus' resurrection shows God's Power
Hope - clinging to Jesus
Come back into union with God
Relationship. Dependency on Jesus

KINGDOM OF DARKNESS

The LORD saw that the wickedness of man was great in the
earth, and that every intention of the thoughts of his heart
was only evil continually. And the LORD regretted that he had
made man on the earth, and it grieved him to his heart.

GENESIS 6:5-6

Adam's sin cost him more than his life. Satan usurped his dominion, and according to Jesus, Satan became "the ruler of this world" (John 14:30). Every archaeological dig of the earliest settlements of humanity reveal pagan worship with animal and human sacrifices. Spiritism was (and still is) the dominant religious orientation in the world. Satan's rule was so pervasive that God was sorry He created mankind.

That may have been the end of human history if Noah hadn't found grace in the eyes of the Lord. The rebirth of humanity through Noah's family didn't fare much better. God had to deliver His people from slavery in Egypt. The Mosaic covenant promised blessings if they kept the law and punishment if they didn't. The fear of punishment can be a deterrent to sin, but it didn't last. So God sent prophets to call the people to repentance, but the prophets were largely ignored and even stoned for their efforts.

The kingdom of darkness will rule over those whose "heart is deceitful above all things, and desperately sick" (Jeremiah 17:9). But God said, "I will give you a new heart, and a new spirit I will put within you" (Ezekiel 36:26).

My response to God is:

God, give me a new heart
and a new spirit.
My life isn't a perfect following
of you. Soften my heart -
by soaking in your love.

8

A NEW COVENANT

This is the covenant that I will make with the house of
Israel after those days, declares the LORD: I will put my law
within them, and I will write it on their hearts. And I will be
their God, and they shall be my people...For I will forgive
their iniquity, and I will remember their sin no more.

JEREMIAH 31:33-34

Paul said "all who rely on works of the law are under a curse" (Galatians 3:10). Not only are we cursed living under the law, but the law has the capacity to stimulate the desire to do that which it intended to prohibit (Romans 7:5). Tell a child he can't go *there*, and the moment you say it, *there* is where he wants to go. God said Adam could eat from any tree in the Garden of Eden but that one! "Is the law then contrary to the promises of God? Certainly not! For if a law had been given that could give life, then righteousness would indeed be by the law" (Galatians 3:21).

The New Covenant is grace based. The law is within us, and the sin that separated us from God is forgiven. The Ten Commandments become promises of hope. Those who repent and live by faith under the covenant of grace will have no other gods before them, and they will not steal, commit adultery, or dishonor their parents.

My response to God is:

_God, you forgave me even before
I asked. You reconciled me
I stutter out my yearning to be free
in response to the cross. melted by
your love, and healed by your
forgiveness_

9

THE GOSPEL

> You who were dead in your trespasses and the uncircumcision
> of your flesh, God made alive together with him, having forgiven
> us all our trespasses, by canceling the record of debt that stood
> against us with its legal demands. This he set aside, nailing it
> to the cross. He disarmed the rulers and authorities and put
> them to open shame, by triumphing over them in him.

COLOSSIANS 2:13-15

The Old Testament reads like a tragedy of epic proportions. "The whole world lies in the power of the evil one" (1 John 5:19), and every inhabitant is spiritually dead. "But when the fullness of time had come, God sent forth his Son" (Galatians 4:4). The last words of Jesus on the cross were "It is finished" (John 19:30). To be finished, He had to accomplish three tasks.

First, "the death he died he died to sin, once for all" (Romans 6:10).

Second, Jesus was resurrected so that we may have new life in Him. What Adam and Eve lost in the fall was life, and Jesus said, "I came that [anyone] may have life and have it abundantly" (John 10:10).

Third, "the reason the Son of God appeared was to destroy the works of the devil" (1 John 3:8). "He has delivered us from the domain of darkness and transferred us to the kingdom of his beloved Son, in whom we have redemption, the forgiveness of sins" (Colossians 1:13-14). Satan and his demons are disarmed.

My response to God is:

Thank you for freeing me from
Chains - abusive relationship !! *
   - alcohol
   Giving me a way out => Jesus
Giving me a man to move the
   mountains => Joel
Satan losing
   his grip

10

FORGIVEN

I will be merciful toward their iniquities, and I will remember their sins no more. In speaking of a new covenant, he makes the first one obsolete.

HEBREWS 8:12-13

An omniscient God can't forget our sins. "Remembering our sins no more" means He will not use our past against us in the future. "As far as the east is from the west, so far does he remove our transgressions from us" (Psalm 103:12). The devil will bring up our past and use it against us, but God won't. What about present and future sins? When Christ died once for all our sins, how many of them were future?

No passage in the Epistles instructs us to ask God to forgive us every time we sin. "If we confess our sins, he is faithful and just to forgive us our sins and to cleanse us from all unrighteousness" (1 John 1:9). We aren't forgiven because we confessed our sins; we're forgiven because Christ took the punishment we deserved on Himself. God is faithful to Himself and His covenant.

Confession means to agree with God, to live in moral agreement with Him, which is cleansing. "My little children, I am writing these things to you so that you may not sin. But if anyone does sin, we have an advocate with the Father, Jesus Christ the righteous. He is the propitiation for our sins" (2:1-2).

My response to God is:

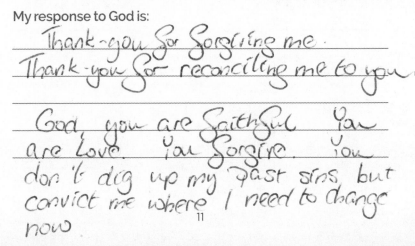

Thank-you for forgiving me.
Thank-you for reconciling me to you.

God, you are faithful. You are Love. You forgive. You don't dig up my past sins but convict me where I need to change now.

11

RECONCILED

God shows his love for us in that while we were still sinners, Christ
died for us. Since, therefore, we have now been justified by his
blood, much more shall we be saved by him from the wrath of God.

ROMANS 5:8-9

Christianity can be separated from any other religion in the world by
asking one question: On what basis are you forgiven and accepted?
We can do nothing and don't have to do anything to qualify for God's
unconditional love and acceptance. While we were still sinners, Christ
died for us. To be *justified* means to be free from blame, just as if we
never sinned. "Since we have been justified by faith, we have peace
with God through our Lord Jesus Christ" (Romans 5:1). It's liberating
to know that we are forgiven, but there is so much more.

"For if while we were enemies we were reconciled to God by the
death of his Son, *much more,* now that we are reconciled, shall we be
saved by his life" (verse 10, emphasis added). Thank God for the cross,
but the resurrection is what we celebrate every Sunday. Good Friday
had to happen, but Easter is eternal life in Christ. "More than that, we
also rejoice in God through our Lord Jesus Christ, through whom we
have now received reconciliation" (verse 11). Eternal life is not something we get when we physically die. We have it now.

My response to God is:

_____

_____

_____

_____

SALVATION

When the goodness and loving kindness of God our Savior
appeared, he saved us, not because of works done by us
in righteousness, but according to his own mercy.

TITUS 3:4-5

Salvation is not about making a bad person a better person. It's about making a dead person a living person. If you had the power and desire to save a dead person, what would you do? Give that person life? If that's all you did, the person would only die again. You have to cure the disease that caused the person to die and then give that person life.

Cryogenics is a branch of science that deals with extremely cold temperatures. Attempts have been made to fast-freeze a corpse with the hopes of resuscitating the person after a cure has been found for the disease that caused death. That is hopeless.

Sin is the "disease" that caused us to die spiritually, and there is only one cure: "Without the shedding of blood there is no forgiveness of sins" (Hebrews 9:22). Blood has two purposes. First, it carries impurities from dying cells and flushes them out through the kidneys. "The blood of Jesus his Son cleanses us from all sin" (1 John 1:7). Second, it brings new life to replace dying cells. Life is in the blood, and Jesus is our life (Colossians 3:3).

My response to God is:

_____

_____

_____

_____

_____

THE ACCUSER

Then he showed me Joshua the high priest standing before the angel of the LORD, and Satan standing at his right hand to accuse him. And the LORD said to Satan, "The LORD rebuke you, O Satan...Is not this a brand plucked from the fire?"

ZECHARIAH 3:1-2

The high priest went through elaborate purification rights before going into the Holy of Holies on the Day of Atonement. Bells were attached to his robe, and a rope was tied to his leg. The rest of the Levites would wait outside and listen for the bells. If they stopped ringing, the rope was there to pull out the dead priest. Nobody else would want to go in before a just God. In Zechariah's vision, Joshua is standing before God in a filthy garment (Zechariah 3:3), and Satan is accusing him.

In the courts of heaven, God the Father is the judge; Satan is the prosecuting attorney; and Jesus is our defense attorney who is standing there with His nail-pierced hands and feet. Jesus has never lost a case. In the vision, the court clerk is an angel, who said, "Behold, I have taken your iniquity away from you, and I will clothe you with pure vestments" (verse 4). Are we not children of God who have been saved from the pits of hell?

My response to God is:

_____

_____

_____

_____

_____

ACCUSATION VERSUS CONVICTION

I rejoice, not because you were grieved, but because you were grieved
into repenting. For you felt a godly grief, so that you suffered no
loss through us. For godly grief produces a repentance that leads
to salvation without regret, whereas worldly grief produces death.

2 CORINTHIANS 7:9-10

The salvation and the power and the kingdom of our God and the authority of his Christ have come, for the accuser of our brothers [and sisters] has been thrown down, who accuses them day and night before our God" (Revelation 12:10). Every believer has struggled with condemning thoughts leaving them feeling guilty. The devil tempts us, and when we fail he relentlessly accuses us day and night. How can we tell the difference between the Holy Spirit convicting us of our sin and Satan accusing us?

The Holy Spirit will convict us when we sin, which should prompt us to confess our sin leading to repentance without regret. This is part of the sanctifying process. However, if we have confessed all known sin yet continue struggling with condemning thoughts, that is the work of the accuser.

Peter betrayed Christ three times, came under the conviction of the Holy Spirit, repented, and became the spokesperson for the early church. Judas Iscariot betrayed Christ, came under Satan's accusations, and hung himself. "There is therefore now no condemnation for those who are in Christ Jesus" (Romans 8:1).

My response to God is:

_____

_____

_____

_____

UNION WITH GOD

To the saints who are in Ephesus, and are faithful in Christ Jesus:
Grace to you and peace from God our Father and the Lord Jesus Christ.

EPHESIANS 1:1-2

Paul always identifies Christians as saints, which refers to our identity in Christ and not necessarily to our maturity. The early church understood salvation to mean union with God, and that is most often portrayed by Paul as being "in Christ," or "in Him," or "in the beloved." Forty such prepositional phrases are in the six chapters of Ephesians. God "has blessed us *in Christ*" (Ephesians 1:3), and He "chose us *in him* before the foundation of the world" (verse 4). "*In him* we have redemption through his blood, the forgiveness of our trespasses" (verse 7). "*In him* we have obtained an inheritance" (verse 11). "*In him* you also, when you heard the word of truth, the gospel of your salvation, and believed *in him*, were sealed with the promised Holy Spirit" (verse 13).

"To them God chose to make known how great among the Gentiles are the riches of the glory of this mystery, which is Christ in you, the hope of glory" (Colossians 1:27). Mystery does not mean mysterious. It refers to something that was not previously known but now is being made known. For every verse in the Bible that mentions Christ being in us are ten verses telling us who we are "in Christ."

My response to God is:

_____

_____

_____

_____

_____

IN CHRIST

From now on, therefore, we regard no one according to the flesh.

2 CORINTHIANS 5:16

Before we came to Christ, we were "in Adam," or "in the flesh." We were identified by our natural heritage and sinful nature. Secular recovery groups have participants introduce themselves by saying, "Hi. I'm Adam, and I'm an alcoholic [or addict or co-dependent]." Paul, however, never identifies believers by their flesh patterns. We are not sinners; we are saints who sin. Pauline theology is all based on who we are "in Christ." He tells the church in Corinth, "That is why I sent you Timothy, my beloved and faithful child in the Lord, to remind you of my ways *in Christ*, as I teach them everywhere in every church" (1 Corinthians 4:17, emphasis added). "You, however, are not in the flesh but in the Spirit, if in fact the Spirit of God dwells in you. Anyone who does not have the Spirit of Christ does not belong to him" (Romans 8:9).

We can't consistently behave in a way that is inconsistent with what we believe about ourselves. What do sinners, alcoholics, and addicts do? They sin! What we do doesn't determine who we are; who we are is what determines what we do. So who are we? "Beloved, we are God's children now…and everyone who thus hopes in him purifies himself as he is pure" (1 John 3:2-3).

My response to God is:

_____

_____

_____

_____

_____

BRIDE OF CHRIST

"Hallelujah! For the Lord our God the Almighty reigns. Let us rejoice and exult and give him the glory, for the marriage of the Lamb has come, and his Bride has made herself ready; it was granted her to clothe herself with fine linen, bright and pure"—for the fine linen is the righteous deeds of the saints.

REVELATION 19:6-8

Suppose you were a prostitute. That is how you saw yourself, and that is how you made your living. Then one day the king offered a decree that all prostitutes would henceforth be forgiven. You saw the decree and believed it. That would be great news, and you would probably celebrate. Would knowing that you were forgiven change your perception of yourself? Would it change your behavior? Probably not, and you would likely go on living as you always had.

What if the decree also said that the king had made you his bride, and you believed it? Would that change your perception of yourself? Would that change how you behave? Beloved, you are the bride of Christ. You can be a part of an "adulterous and sinful generation" (Mark 8:38) that is ashamed of Jesus, or you can be wed to Christ, who has done everything the groom needs to do to "present the church to himself in splendor, without spot or wrinkle…that she might be holy and without blemish" (Ephesians 5:27).

My response to God is:

_____

_____

_____

_____

_____

ACCEPTED

Whoever thus serves Christ is acceptable to God and approved by men.
So then let us pursue what makes for peace and for mutual upbuilding.

ROMANS 14:18-19

N othing feels worse than the sting of rejection. Nothing warms the soul more than to be unconditionally loved and accepted. You are loved and accepted, because the moment you received Christ, He gave you "the right to become [a child] of God" (John 1:12). You are God's chosen friend (15:15-16). You "have peace with God through our Lord Jesus Christ" (Romans 5:1). You are united to the Lord and are "one spirit with him" (1 Corinthians 6:17). "Do you not know that your body is a temple of the Holy Spirit within you, whom you have from God" (verse 19).

"You were bought with a price. So glorify God in your body" (verse 20). You have been chosen and adopted as God's child (Ephesians 1:4-5). You have direct access to God the Father through the Holy Spirit (2:18). You are redeemed and forgiven (Colossians 1:14). "You are a chosen race, a royal priesthood, a holy nation, a people for his own possession, that you may proclaim the excellencies of him who called you out of darkness into his marvelous light. Once you were not a people, but now you are God's people; once you had not received mercy, but now you have received mercy" (1 Peter 1:9-10). You are accepted "in Christ."

My response to God is:

_____

_____

_____

_____

_____

SECURE

Who is God, but the LORD? And who is a rock, except God?—the God who equipped me with strength and made my way blameless. He made my feet like the feet of a deer and set me secure on the heights.

PSALM 18:31-33

Gated communities. Home invasion security systems. Smoke and fire alarms. Health, dental, and life insurance. Job security. Identity theft security. None of those guarantee inner security. Your only real security is your eternal life in Christ. "We have this as a sure and steadfast anchor of the soul, a hope that enters into the inner place behind the curtain, where Jesus has gone as a forerunner on our behalf" (Hebrews 6:19-20).

You are assured that "all things work together for good, for those who are called according to his purpose" (Romans 8:28). You are free from any condemning charges brought against you (verse 31 and following). You cannot be separated from the love of God (verse 35 and following). You have been established, anointed, and sealed by God, who has given you His Spirit in your hearts as a guarantee (2 Corinthians 1:21-22). "Your life is hidden with Christ in God" (Colossians 3:3). Your "citizenship is in heaven" (Philippians 3:20). God has not given you a spirit "of fear but of power and love and self-control" (2 Timothy 1:7). You are born of God, and the evil one cannot touch you (1 John 5:18). You are secure "in Christ."

My response to God is:

_____

_____

_____

_____

_____

SIGNIFICANT

I have fought the good fight, I have finished the race, I have kept the
faith. Henceforth there is laid up for me the crown of righteousness,
which the Lord, the righteous judge, will award to me on that day,
and not only to me but also to all who have loved his appearing.

2 TIMOTHY 4:7-8

Who won the World Series, the Oscar for best motion picture, and the Miss America contest ten years ago? What is forgotten in time is of little significance. What will be remembered for eternity is significant. There is joy in heaven when even one sinner repents (Luke 15:7). No child of God is insignificant. "You are the salt of the earth" (Matthew 5:13). "You are the light of the world" (verse 14). "You did not choose me, but I chose you and appointed you that you should go and bear fruit and that your fruit should abide" (John 15:16).

"Do you not know that you are God's temple and that God's Spirit dwells in you?" (1 Corinthians 3:16). You are an ambassador for Christ, who has given you the ministry of reconciliation (2 Corinthians 5:18,20). You are God's coworker (6:1). You are seated with Christ in the heavenlies (Ephesians 2:6). You are God's "workmanship, created in Christ Jesus for good works" (verse 10). You can do all things through Him who strengthens you (Philippians 4:13). You may approach God with confidence (Ephesians 3:12). You are significant "in Christ."

My response to God is:

_____

_____

_____

_____

_____

WE HAVE BEEN SAVED

Christ, having appeared once to bear the sins of many,
will appear a second time, not to deal with sin but to
save those who are eagerly waiting for him.

HEBREWS 9:28

The word *salvation* in Scripture occurs in the past, present, and future tenses. Born-again believers have been saved, are being saved, and someday will be fully saved. "By grace you *have been saved* through faith" (Ephesians 2:8, emphasis added; see also 2 Timothy 1:8-9 and Titus 3:4-5). "Examine yourselves, to see whether you are in the faith. Test yourselves. Or do you not realize this about yourselves, that Jesus Christ is in you?—unless indeed you fail to meet the test!" (2 Corinthians 13:5). "This is the testimony, that God gave us eternal life, and this life is in his Son. Whoever has the Son has life; whoever does not have the Son of God does not have life. I write these things to you who believe in the name of the Son of God, that you may know that you have eternal life" (1 John 5:11-13).

"In him you also, when you heard the word of truth, the gospel of your salvation, and believed in him, were sealed with the promised Holy Spirit [past], who is the guarantee of our inheritance until we acquire possession of it [future]" (Ephesians 1:13-14). There can be no surer guarantee of the consummation of our salvation than the presence of God in our lives.

My response to God is:

_____

_____

_____

_____

_____

WE ARE BEING SAVED

The word of the cross is folly to those who are perishing,
but to us who are *being saved* it is the power of God.

1 CORINTHIANS 1:18 (EMPHASIS ADDED)

God saved His people from the Egyptians as they crossed the Red Sea, but they were not yet in the Promised Land, and neither are we. "Thanks be to God, who in Christ always leads us in triumphal procession, and through us spreads the fragrance of the knowledge of him everywhere. For we are the aroma of Christ to God among those who are *being saved* and among those who are perishing" (2 Corinthians 2:14-15, emphasis added).

We have not yet experienced the totality of our salvation, and we won't until we are fully in the presence of God. On our way to heaven, we will face many obstacles that will challenge our faith. "Therefore, my beloved, as you have always obeyed, so now, not only as in my presence but much more in my absence, work out your own salvation with fear and trembling, for it is God who works in you, both to will and to work for his good pleasure" (Philippians 2:12-13).

We do not work for our salvation; we work out what God has born in us. We don't have a cloud by day and a pillar of fire by night, but we do have the Holy Spirit, who empowers and guides us to our final destination.

My response to God is:

_____

_____

_____

_____

_____

POSITIONAL SANCTIFICATION

This is the will of God, your sanctification.

1 THESSALONIANS 4:3

Adam and Eve were created in the image and likeness of God (Genesis 1:26). Paul admonished us "to put on the new self, created after the likeness of God in true righteousness and holiness" (Ephesians 4:24). Sanctification is the process of becoming like God in righteousness and holiness, and that is God's will for our lives.

Sanctification has three tenses: past, present, and future. We have been sanctified, and we are being sanctified. The sanctifying process began at our new birth and is complete when we are fully in God's presence. Past tense sanctification is often referred to as positional sanctification. "You were washed, *you were sanctified, you were justified* in the name of the Lord Jesus Christ and by the Spirit of our God" (1 Corinthians 6:11, emphasis added). Justification is always past tense for believers. Positional sanctification is just a beginning. "If we say we have no sin, we deceive ourselves, and the truth is not in us" (1 John 1:8). However, "having sin" and "being sin" are two different issues.

At salvation we were set apart or separated unto God, and we participate in God's holiness. "His divine power has granted to us all things that pertain to life and godliness" (2 Peter 1:3). Nothing nor anyone, and not even Satan, can keep us from being the person God created us to be.

My response to God is:

_____

_____

_____

_____

_____

PROGRESSIVE SANCTIFICATION

Since we have these promises, beloved, let us cleanse
ourselves from every defilement of body and spirit, bringing
holiness [sanctification] to completion in the fear of God.

2 CORINTHIANS 7:1

We can overemphasize positional sanctification and believe we are completely sanctified, which will lead to hypocrisy. If we think we have no sin, we should ask our spouses if they agree with us. The other error is to equate sanctification with spiritual growth and dismiss positional sanctification as just positional truth, as though our position in Christ has no present and practical reality. Those who do that spend the rest of their lives trying to become somebody they already are.

Positional sanctification is the basis for progressive sanctification. We are not trying to become children of God; we are children of God who are in the process of becoming more and more like Christ. "Now that you have been set free from sin and have become slaves of God, the benefit you reap leads to holiness [sanctification], and the result is eternal life" (Romans 6:22 NIV).

In justification, God declares the believer righteous, because the righteousness of Christ is accounted to the believer. Sanctification is the gracious and continuous work of the Holy Spirit to deliver believers from the pollution of sin, transforming them by the renewing of their minds to be like Christ, enabling them to do good works to the glory of God. Sanctification is the present focus of God's work in us.

My response to God is:

_____

_____

_____

_____

_____

PROCLAMATION OF EMANCIPATION

For freedom Christ has set us free; stand firm therefore,
and do not submit again to a yoke of slavery.

GALATIANS 5:1

Slavery in the United States was abolished by the Thirteenth Amendment to our constitution on December 18, 1865. How many slaves were there in the United States on December 19? None. But how many still lived like slaves? Slave owners had no legal right over them, but if they could keep them from knowing the truth, their control over them wouldn't be challenged. As long as slaves continued to do what slaves do, it wouldn't be hard to convince them that they were still slaves. The unbelieving slave still felt like he was in bondage and didn't want to be hypocritical, so he continued to live according to how he felt.

One former slave heard the good news and received it with joy. He confirmed that the proclamation was authorized by the highest of authorities and discovered that it was the authority figure Himself who personally paid the price for his freedom. He correctly reasoned it would be hypocritical to believe his feelings and not believe the truth. His life was transformed. His old master no longer had any authority over him and did not need to be obeyed. The former slave gladly served the one who set him free.

"Sin will have no dominion over you, since you are not under law but under grace" (Romans 6:14). Grace costs us nothing, but it cost Christ everything.

My response to God is:

_____

_____

_____

_____

TRANSFORMED

Do not be conformed to this world, but be transformed by the
renewal of your mind, that by testing you may discern what is
the will of God, what is good and acceptable and perfect.

ROMANS 12:2

If we have been transferred out of the domain of darkness into the
kingdom of God's beloved Son (Colossians 1:13), and if we are no longer "in Adam" but are alive and free "in Christ," why do we often think
and feel the way we did before salvation? Before we came to Christ, we
were all conformed to this world. Our souls were not in union with
God, and we had no knowledge of God and His ways. We learned to
live independently of Him. This learned independence is the essential
characteristic of what the Bible calls the flesh, or old nature.

Then one day we chose to believe God and received Christ as our
Lord and Savior. "Therefore, if anyone is in Christ, he is a new creation.
The old has passed away; behold, the new has come" (2 Corinthians
5:17). However, everything that was programmed into our minds is
still there, and there is no delete button. We can continue being conformed to this world, or we can be transformed by the renewing of our
minds. "Do your best to present yourself to God as one approved, a
worker who has no need to be ashamed, rightly handling the word of
truth" (2 Timothy 2:15).

My response to God is:

_____

_____

_____

_____

_____

FAITH

Faith is the assurance of things hoped for,
the conviction of things not seen.

HEBREWS 11:1

We are saved by faith (Ephesians 2:8), sanctified by faith (Acts 26:18), and live by faith (Romans 1:17). Every aspect of the Christian life is related to faith. *Faith, believe,* and *trust* all come from the same root word, with *faith* being a noun, whereas *believe* and *trust* are interchangeable verbs. To believe in something or somebody is more than just giving mental ascent. It's a demonstrated reliance on something or somebody. To say you believe in somebody is the same as saying you trust that person and then live as though you really do. Faith is a firm persuasion or conviction based on hearing. Paul wrote, "I am not ashamed, for I know whom I have believed, and I am convinced that he is able to guard until that day" (2 Timothy 1:12).

James asks, "What good is it...if someone says he has faith but does not have works? Can that faith save him?" (James 2:14). No, it can't. If what we profess to believe doesn't affect our walk and our talk, then we don't really believe. We can tell what a person believes by how they live. People don't always live according to what they profess, but they do live according to what they really believe. "The righteous shall live by faith" (Romans 1:17).

My response to God is:

_____

_____

_____

_____

_____

RULES OF FAITH

Everyone who has been born of God overcomes the world.
And this is the victory that has overcome the world—our faith.

1 JOHN 5:4

Faith is the operating principle of life. Everybody lives by faith. The real question is in what or in whom we believe. Three rules govern Christian faith. First, faith has to have an object. There is no such thing as faith in faith. The object of faith in the New Testament is always God, Christ, or things spiritual. To step out in faith beyond what we know to be true is not faith but presumption.

Second, how much faith we have is dependent on how well we know the object of our faith. If we know seven biblical promises, the best we can have is a seven-promise faith. If we know seven thousand promises, we can have that much more faith. The heroes of faith mentioned in Hebrews chapter 11 had great faith because they knew and believed in a great God. The more we come to know God and His ways, the more we expand our faith. "Faith comes from hearing, and hearing through the word of Christ" (Romans 10:17).

Third, faith that isn't acted on isn't faith at all. "Without faith it is impossible to please him, for whoever would draw near to God must believe that he exists and that he rewards those who seek him" (Hebrews 11:6).

My response to God is:

_____

_____

_____

_____

_____

KNOWING GOD

Whatever gain I had, I counted as loss for the sake of
Christ. Indeed, I count everything as loss because of the
surpassing worth of knowing Christ Jesus my Lord.

PHILIPPIANS 3:7-8

Paul was a rising star in Judaism who had knowledge about the God
of Abraham, Isaac, and Jacob, but he didn't know Him personally
until the Lord struck him down on the road to Damascus (Acts 9:1 and
following). The Westminster Confession says, "God is a Spirit, infinite, eternal, and unchanging in His being, wisdom, power, holiness,
justice, goodness and truth." "How great is God—beyond our understanding! The number of his years is past finding out" (Job 36:26 NIV).
Being finite, we cannot fully comprehend the infinite, yet we can truly
know God as our heavenly Father. Paul prayed "that the God of our
Lord Jesus Christ, the Father of glory, may give you the Spirit of wisdom and of revelation in the knowledge of him" (Ephesians 1:17).

Jesus said, "Whoever has seen me has seen the Father" (John 14:9).
It is through Christ that we personally know our heavenly Father. "No
one knows the Son except the Father, and no one knows the Father
except the Son and anyone to whom the Son chooses to reveal him"
(Matthew 11:27). Knowing God and who we are in relationship to
Him is the bedrock of our faith. Having a personal relationship with
the King of kings is the ultimate privilege.

My response to God is:

_____

_____

_____

_____

_____

MENTAL HEALTH

You keep him in perfect peace whose mind is
stayed on you, because he trusts in you.

ISAIAH 26:3

Psychologists and psychiatrists define mental health as being in touch with reality and relatively free of anxiety. Any of their clients who are under assault by the evil one would fail on both counts. Therapists don't see and hear what those clients are experiencing, and anxiety disorders almost always accompany spiritual conflicts.

Christians have a different perspective. The ultimate reality is God, and being in touch with Him is the basis for mental health. Nothing exists without the Creator who "upholds the universe by the word of his power" (Hebrews 1:3). Mentally healthy people have a true knowledge of God and a true understanding of themselves. Would people be mentally healthy if they knew the enemy was disarmed and that God loved them, forgave them, and set them free from their past by making them new creations "in Christ," meeting all their needs according to His riches in glory? And that he has prepared a place for them in eternity, and that the peace of God is guarding their hearts and their minds "in Christ Jesus"? And if they could cast all their anxieties on Him?

Many people deemed mentally ill have a distorted concept of God and of themselves. Since many patients in mental hospitals exhibit religious tendencies, secular therapists conclude that religion is part of their problem, when a true relationship with God may be their only hope.

My response to God is:

_____

_____

_____

_____

_____

GOD IS HOLY

Exalt the LORD our God, and worship at his holy
mountain; for the LORD our God is holy!

PSALM 99:9

No other attribute in the Bible speaks more directly to God's deity than His holiness. "The Holy One" (Hosea 11:9) is distinct and separate from all other things. He is "exalted over all the nations" (Psalm 99:2 NIV) and lives above and beyond all creation. The stain of sin and evil that defiled the world never had any effect on God. He has always been morally perfect and separate (or transcendent) from the rest of His fallen creation. "The holy God shows himself holy in righteousness" (Isaiah 5:16).

The prophet Isaiah was given a vision of God seated on a throne. Above the throne were seraphim calling out to one another, "Holy, holy, holy is the LORD of hosts; the whole earth is full of his glory!" (6:3). Confronted with God's holiness, Isaiah cried out, "Woe is me! For I am lost; for I am a man of unclean lips, and I dwell in the midst of a people of unclean lips; for my eyes have seen the King, the LORD of hosts!" (verse 5). We would all fall on our faces if such a manifestation of God were to come upon us. The only sin we would be aware of is our own. When we distance ourselves from God, we are less aware of our own sins and more aware of other people's sins.

My response to God is:

_____

_____

_____

_____

_____

THE GLORY OF GOD

Ascribe to the LORD, O heavenly beings, ascribe to the LORD
glory and strength. Ascribe to the LORD the glory due his
name; worship the LORD in the splendor of holiness.

PSALM 29:1-2

The sheer magnitude of God's glory and greatness does not diminish over time. Familiarity does not breed contempt of the Almighty. The holy angels, who have been in His presence since their creation, day and night do not cease to proclaim, "Holy, holy, holy, is the Lord God Almighty, who was and is and is to come!" (Revelation 4:8).

No mortal can fully grasp the glory of God, although Moses came closer than anyone else. Moses said to God, "Please show me your glory" (Exodus 33:18). The Lord responded by placing Moses in the cleft of a rock and allowing His glory to pass by him. God covered Moses's face "for man shall not see [God] and live" (verse 20). When Moses came down from the mountain, "the skin of his face shone" (34:29), which slowly faded away. The *Shekinah* (literally, "that which dwells") glory is a manifestation of God's presence. It was present in the Holy of Holies, but progressively departed from Israel until "the Word became flesh and dwelt among us, and we have seen his glory, glory as of the only Son from the Father, full of grace and truth" (John 1:14). To "glorify God in your body" (1 Corinthians 6:20) is to manifest the presence of God.

My response to God is:

_____

_____

_____

_____

_____

WORSHIP

The hour is coming, and is now here, when the true
worshipers will worship the Father in spirit and truth, for
the Father is seeking such people to worship him.

JOHN 4:23

Seeing a ten-foot giant a mile away may catch your eye but solicit little response. Standing toe-to-toe with the giant would probably provoke fear and awe. You wouldn't say "Praise you," but you probably would say or think, *This man is huge!* Nobody would be forcing you to respond that way.

To worship God is to ascribe to Him His divine attributes. If you were ushered into His presence, nobody would force you to worship Him, but you would. You wouldn't be able to help yourself. You would be so overwhelmed that you would probably be speechless and in absolute awe of Him.

God doesn't need us to tell Him who He is. We are the ones who need to consciously keep the divine attributes of God in our minds. He is looking for worshippers who live as though He really is omnipresent. Who ascribe to His omnipotence and believe this: "I can do all things through him who strengthens me" (Philippians 4:13). Who ascribe to God's omniscience, and when they lack wisdom, "ask God who gives generously to all without reproach" (James 1:5). Who "love one another for love is from God, and whoever loves has been born of God and knows God" (1 John 4:7).

My response to God is:

_____

_____

_____

_____

_____

GOD IS OMNIPRESENT

If I ascend to heaven, you are there! If I make my bed in
Sheol, you are there! If I take the wings of the morning, and
dwell in the uttermost parts of the sea, even there your
hand shall lead me, and your right hand shall hold me.

PSALM 139:8-10

God is everywhere present, even for non-believers: "What can be known about God is plain to them, because God has shown it to them. For his invisible attributes, namely, his eternal power and divine nature, have been clearly perceived, ever since the creation of the world, in the things that have been made. So they are without excuse" (Romans 1:19-20).

God is also present with every believer, but we are only partially present with Him even though our bodies are His temple. We don't always sense His presence because of the daily responsibilities that occupy our minds. It's possible to be so heavenly minded that we are no earthly good. A sinful lifestyle and unresolved conflicts will diminish a sense of His presence. Consciously or subconsciously, we have distanced ourselves from God, but He has not distanced Himself from us. He "will never leave you nor forsake you" (Hebrews 13:5).

A peaceful sense of His presence comes when we repent and believe again that He is present and live accordingly. David said, "I have set the LORD always before me; because he is at my right hand, I shall not be shaken" (Psalm 16:8).

My response to God is:

_____

_____

_____

_____

_____

THE POWER OF HIS PRESENCE

My presence will go with you, and I will give you rest.

EXODUS 33:14

God saddled Moses with the responsibility of leading His people to the Promised Land. Feeling overwhelmed by the responsibility, Moses asked God the two most important questions any spiritual leader can ask: *Who is going with me?* and *Will you please show me your ways "that I may know you in order to find favor in your sight?"* (Exodus 33:12-13). God's work done in God's way will never lack God's support. Trying to serve God in our own strength and resources will lead to burnout.

Wandering around in the wilderness for 40 years with no bathroom facilities is not anybody's idea of rest, and yet God did give Moses rest. The only way you can ascertain whether an event was restful is by how you feel when it's over. "Moses was 120 years old when he died. His eye was undimmed, and his vigor was unabated" (Deuteronomy 34:7). "There remains a Sabbath rest for the people of God, for whoever has entered God's rest has also rested from his works as God did from his" (Hebrews 4:9-10). The Sabbath rest is living by faith in the power of His presence. God has a way of bringing us to the end of our resources, and out of our brokenness we discover His. "Not by might, nor by power, but by my Spirit, says the LORD of hosts" (Zechariah 4:6).

My response to God is:

_____

_____

_____

_____

_____

COME TO HIS PRESENCE

Come to me, all who labor and are heavy laden, and I will give you rest. Take my yoke upon you, and learn from me, for I am gentle and lowly of heart, and you will find rest for your souls. For my yoke is easy, and my burden is light.

MATTHEW 11:28-30

Jesus was a carpenter in His youth, and He probably fashioned yokes and doors, which became metaphors for coming into His presence (John 10:9). Yokes are heavy beams that fit over the shoulders of two oxen. They work only if two creatures are in them and pulling together. Young ox are trained by yoking them together with an older ox who "learned obedience through what he suffered" (Hebrews 5:8). Some young ox think the pace is too slow, so they try to run on ahead. Some just want to drop out, and life becomes a drag. Others are tempted to stray off to the left or the right and are a pain in the neck.

Wise "young oxen" think, *This old ox knows how to walk. I think I will learn from him.* They learn to not only take one day at a time, but the priority of relationships. They learn to walk with God. "Young men shall fall exhausted; but they who wait for the LORD shall renew their strength; they shall mount up with wings like eagles; they shall run and not be weary; they shall walk and not faint" (Isaiah 40:30-31).

My response to God is:

_____

_____

_____

_____

_____

ALMIGHTY GOD

Hallelujah! For the Lord our God the Almighty reigns.

REVELATION 19:6

The adjective *omnipotent* is rendered "Almighty" in Scripture and occurs only in the book of Revelation and in 2 Corinthians 6:18. Only the Almighty has the power to create something out of nothing and rule the universe. In the Gospels, we see that Jesus demonstrated His power over nature and the spiritual realm.

God's power was uniquely demonstrated on a personal level in granting the barren Elizabeth to be pregnant with John the Baptist and in miracuously impregnating the Virgin Mary so that Jesus could rightfully sit on the throne of David (Luke 1:26-38). When the astonished Mary asked how this could be, "The angel answered her, 'The Holy Spirit will come upon you, and the power of the Most High will overshadow you...For nothing will be impossible with God'" (verses 35,37).

Paul prays that the eyes of our hearts may be enlightened so that we will know "what is the immeasureable greatness of his power toward us who believe" (Ephesians 1:19). Imagine what that means since our souls are in union with Almighty God. Paul said, "For this I toil, struggling with all his energy that he powerfully works within me" (Colossians 1:29); "I can do all things through him who strenthens me" (Philippians 4:13); and "Now to him who is able to do far more abundantly than all that we ask or think, according to the power at work within us" (Ephesians 3:20).

My response to God is:

_____

_____

_____

_____

GOD KNOWS EVERYTHING

You, Solomon my son, know the God of your father and serve
him with a whole heart and with a willing mind, for the LORD
searches all hearts and understands every plan and thought.

1 CHRONICLES 28:9

God knew us from eternity past (Ephesians 2:10), and "for those whom he foreknew he also predestined to be conformed to the image of his Son" (Romans 8:29). "No creature is hidden from his sight, but all are naked and exposed to the eyes of him to whom we must give an account" (Hebrews 4:13). Since God knows the "thoughts and intentions of the heart" (verse 12), we can silently commune with our heavenly Father. But this also means that any act of sin is known before it is committed. Secret sin on earth is open scandal in heaven.

We understand the successive events of time and reason accordingly, but God sees the past, present, and future simultaneously. For God everything is "one eternal now." His foreknowledge necessitates some degree of predetermination, but even though God is sovereign, we have the freedom to choose. In ways we cannot fully understand, God participates with humanity in making legitimately free choices in such a way that He can know for certain the outcome.

God's omniscience is a tremendous blessing for believers. First, the Holy Spirit who guides us knows the future. Second, because of our union with God "we have the mind of Christ" (1 Corinthians 2:16).

My response to God is:

_____

_____

_____

_____

_____

TEST THE SPIRIT

For such men are false apostles, deceitful workmen, disguising
themselves as apostles of Christ. And no wonder, for even
Satan disguises himself as an angel of light. So it is no surprise
if his servants, also, disguise themselves as servants of
righteousness. Their end will correspond to their deeds.

2 CORINTHIANS 11:13-15

Beginning in the Garden of Eden and continuing through the book of Revelation, the Bible depicts a battle between good and evil, between the kingdom of God and the kingdom of darkness, between true prophets and false prophets, between good angels and evil spirits, between the Spirit of truth and the father of lies, between Christ and the anti-Christ. God never disguises Himself, and He does everything overtly in the light. By definition, the occult means hidden, and deceitful workmen operate covertly. Satan's first strategy is to remain undetected, but when exposed he reverts to a pretense of power. Almost all occultic activity is centered around the human mind and the future, giving the illusion that Satan, like God, has perfect knowledge of both.

We should never ascribe to Satan the divine attributes of God. Although we should not be ignorant of Satan's schemes (2 Corinthians 2:11), the goal is to know God and His ways, and then the counterfeit becomes evident. "Let him who boasts boast in this, that he understands and knows me, that I am the LORD who practices steadfast love, justice, and righteousness in the earth" (Jeremiah 9:24).

My response to God is:

_____

_____

_____

_____

_____

GOD IS LOVE

Whoever confesses that Jesus is the Son of God, God abides
in him, and he in God. So we have come to know and to
believe the love that God has for us. God is love, and whoever
abides in love abides in God, and God abides in him.

1 JOHN 4:15-16

The Greek word *phileo* means brotherly love and refers to the natural affection we show one another. The Greek word *agape* refers to the character of God and is not dependent on the object. God loves us because it is His nature to love us. That is why the love of God is unconditional. "If you love those who love you, what credit is that to you? For even sinners love those who love them" (Luke 6:32 NASB).

When first attracted to our spouses, we fall in love (*phileo*) with them. We love them because of who they are. As we grow in the grace and knowledge of the Lord Jesus Christ, we learn to love (*agape*) them because of who we are. That is what Paul had in mind when he wrote, "Husbands, love your wives, as Christ loved the church and gave himself up for her" (Ephesians 5:25). To say we don't love someone says more about us than it does about the other person. "The goal of our instruction is love from a pure heart and a good conscience and a sincere faith" (1 Timothy 1:5 NASB).

My response to God is:

_____

_____

_____

_____

_____

LOVING ONE ANOTHER

By this we know love, that he laid down his life for us, and we
ought to lay down our lives for the brothers. But if anyone has
the world's goods and sees his brother in need, yet closes his
heart against him, how does God's love abide in him? Little
children, let us not love in word or talk but in deed and in truth.

1 JOHN 3:16-18

Love (*agape*) is a noun and refers to the character of God. "Love is
patient and kind; love does not envy or boast; it is not arrogant or
rude. It does not insist on its own way; it is not irritable or resentful; it
does not rejoice at wrongdoing, but rejoices with the truth. Love bears
all things, believes all things, hopes all things, endures all things. Love
never ends" (1 Corinthians 13:4-8). *Agapao* is a verb and refers to the
action taken by those who sacrificially love one another. The love of
God compels us to meet one another's needs.

Paul prayed that you "be strengthened with power through his
Spirit in your inner being, so that Christ may dwell in your hearts
through faith—that you, being rooted and grounded in love, may have
strength to comprehend with all the saints what is the breadth and
length and height and depth, and to know the love of Christ that sur-
passes knowledge, that you may be filled with all the fullness of God"
(Ephesians 3:16-19).

My response to God is:

_____

_____

_____

_____

_____

GOD IS GOOD

The LORD is good and his love endures forever.

PSALM 100:5 NIV

Jesus said, "There is only one who is good" (Matthew 19:17). Therefore, everything God does is good, and we are the benefactors. "We know that for those who love God all things work together for good, for those who are called according to his purpose" (Romans 8:28). The problem is we don't always know what's good for us. What tastes good is often unhealthy. What looks good might be so in appearance only, and what might at first appear to be bad might not be. Joseph said to his brothers who betrayed him, "You intended to harm me, but God intended it for good to accomplish what is now being done" (Genesis 50:20 NIV).

If God is all-powerful and good, then why do bad things happen to good people? It's impossible to answer that question unless we understand evil forces are actively opposing the will of God. "Yet you say, 'The way of the Lord is not just.' Hear now, O house of Israel: Is my way not just? Is it not your ways that are not just?" (Ezekiel 18:25). "Have I any pleasure in the death of the wicked, declares the Lord GOD, and not rather that he should turn from his way and live?" (verse 23).

God is the author of life, not death, and He is making right what His rebellious creation has made wrong.

My response to God is:

_____

_____

_____

_____

_____

GOD IS MERCIFUL

When the goodness and loving kindness of God our Savior
appeared, he saved us, not because of works done by us
in righteousness, but according to his own mercy.

TITUS 3:4-5

Blessed are they who observe justice, who do righteousness at all times!" (Psalm 106:3). But we don't always do righteousness. Justice is rightness and fairness. God is always just and cannot be otherwise. Justice is carried out when people get what they deserve. If God gave us what we deserve, we would all be sentenced to hell.

Thankfully, God is also merciful, and "for our sake he made [Christ] to be sin who knew no sin, so that in him we might become the righteousness of God" (2 Corinthians 5:21). Mercy is not giving someone what they deserve. When we throw ourselves on the mercy of the court, we're saying, "I am guilty, but please be lenient and don't give me what I deserve." Grace is giving other people what they don't deserve.

What we have freely received from God we are to freely give to others. "We love because he first loved us" (1 John 4:19). "Be kind to one another, tenderhearted, forgiving one another, as God in Christ forgave you" (Ephesians 4:32). "Be merciful, even as your Father is merciful" (Luke 6:36). In other words, don't give people what they deserve, but, also, don't stop there. Be gracious and give them what they don't deserve. Love one another.

My response to God is:

_____

_____

_____

_____

_____

THE GRACE OF GOD

Let us then with confidence draw near to the throne of grace,
that we may receive mercy and find grace to help in time of need.

HEBREWS 4:16

Secular programs can appear to be more merciful and less judgmental than many church programs because they have no moral standard to uphold. We have the grace to help in time of need, but if we don't first show mercy, we might never have the opportunity. One act of unkindness or hostile criticism, and the seeker shuts down. People don't share their burdens with someone who can't relate to them or understand their situation, nor do they unburden themselves to those who are unable to help them.

A Wonderful Counselor meets that criteria. "We do not have a high priest who is unable to sympathize with our weaknesses, but one who in every respect has been tempted as we are, yet without sin" (Hebrews 4:15). Sinners loved to be around Jesus, but He was critical of the Pharisees, who, He said, "tie up heavy burdens, hard to bear, and lay them on people's shoulders, but they themselves are not willing to move them with their finger" (Matthew 23:4).

Living under the New Covenant of grace is not a license to sin, and only by the grace of God do we not sin. God's grace is a holy enablement: "My grace is sufficient for you, for my power is perfected in weakness" (2 Corinthians 12:9).

My response to God is:

_____

_____

_____

_____

_____

GOD IS FAITHFUL

I will sing of the steadfast love of the LORD, forever; with my mouth I will make known your faithfulness to all generations.

PSALM 89:1

From the time God made a covenant with Abraham in Genesis 12:1-3, His unlikely promises were slowly but progressively fulfilled despite overwhelming odds, even when they seemed humanly impossible. The Messianic line began with Sarah, who gave birth to Isaac when, humanly, she could no longer bear children. Then God provided a scapegoat to take the place of Isaac when he was ordered to be sacrificed, preserving Abraham and Sarah's posterity. God promised that the seed of the woman would continue through the house of David and that the Messiah would sit on the throne of David. "Once for all I have sworn by my holiness; I will not lie to David. His offspring shall endure forever, his throne as long as the sun before me. Like the moon it shall be established forever, a faithful witness in the skies" (Psalm 89:35-37).

Pharaoh tried to prevent the birth of Moses, the law giver, by ordering that every son born to a Hebrew woman be "cast into the Nile" (Exodus 1:22). Herod ordered all males two years old and younger to be killed to prevent the birth of Christ, the law fulfiller. Only a fool would trust someone who is unreliable, so expect the ruler of this world and his subjects to try to chip away at our realization of God's faithfulness.

My response to God is:

_____

_____

_____

_____

_____

GOD IS IMMUTABLE

God is not man, that he should lie, or a son of man, that
he should change his mind. Has he said, and will he not
do it? Or has he spoken, and will he not fulfill it?

NUMBERS 23:19

The grass withers, the flower fades, but the word of our God will stand forever" (Isaiah 40:8). The word and character of God never change, and that is in stark contrast to humanity, which is in a constant state of flux. The changeless nature of God is what makes Him the ultimate object of our faith. The writer of Hebrews said, "Remember your leaders, those who spoke to you the word of God. Consider the outcome of their way of life, and imitate their faith. Jesus Christ is the same yesterday and today and forever" (Hebrews 13:7-8). The passage doesn't say to imitate the behavior of those who lead us. But if they are bearing the fruit of righteousness, then imitate what they believe.

The most reliable object of faith for pagans is the fixed order of the universe. That's why many are sun worshippers and astrologers who believe they can foretell the fate of nations and the fortunes of people by the movements of heavenly bodies. More people know their astrological sign and read their daily horoscope than daily read God's Word. "They exchanged the truth about God for a lie and worshipped and served the creature rather than the Creator" (Romans 1:25).

My response to God is:

_____

_____

_____

_____

_____

THE TRINITY

Go therefore and make disciples of all nations, baptizing them in
the name of the Father and of the Son and of the Holy Spirit.

MATTHEW 28:19

"Hear O Israel: The LORD our God, the LORD is one" (Deuteronomy 6:4). Old Testament Judaism and New Testament Christianity both teach monotheism (one God) as opposed to polytheism (many gods), pantheism (all is God), or atheism (no god or gods). Only Christianity recognizes the divine three-in-oneness—the eternal coexistence of the Father, Son, and Holy Spirit in the inner personal life of the Godhead. Notice the use of plural pronouns when God said, "Let us make mankind in our image, in our likeness" (Genesis 1:26 NIV). We are united to all three at salvation: "You, however, are not in the flesh but in the Spirit, if in fact the Spirit of God dwells in you. Anyone who does not have the Spirit of Christ does not belong to him" (Romans 8:9).

In the High Priestly Prayer, Jesus asks that we be kept "from the evil one" (John 17:15), who seeks to divide our minds, marriages, and ministries. The Trinity is the perfect model of unity that Jesus prays will be the case for us: "[I ask] that they may all be one, just as you, Father, are in me, and I in you, that they also may be in us, so that the world may believe that you have sent me" (verses 20-21).

My response to God is:

_____

_____

_____

_____

_____

I AM WHO I AM

I told you that you would die in your sins, for unless
you believe that I am he you will die in your sins.

JOHN 8:24

God said to Moses, 'I am who I am'" (Exodus 3:14). "This is my name forever, and thus I am to be remembered throughout all generations" (verse 15). God is the eternal now. The most distinctive name for God is Yahweh (Jehovah), which comes from the same root as "I am." This name was given to convince the children of Israel that God was faithful to His covenant and would lead them out of bondage.

Jesus came to lead us out of bondage to sin, and He said to the Jews, "Truly, truly I say to you, before Abraham was, *I am*" (John 8:58, emphasis added as with the following). "*I am* the bread of life" (6:48). "*I am* the resurrection and the life. Whoever believes in me, though he die [physically], yet shall he live [spiritually]" (11:25). "Truly, truly, I say to you, *I am* the door of the sheep" (10:7). "*I am* the way, and the truth, and the life. No one comes to the Father except through me" (14:6). "*I am* the good shepherd. The good shepherd lays down his life for the sheep" (10:11). "There is salvation in no one else, for there is no other name under heaven given among men by which we must be saved" (Acts 4:12).

My response to God is:

_____

_____

_____

_____

_____

THE LAST ADAM

The first man Adam became a living being;
the last Adam became a life-giving spirit.

1 CORINTHIANS 15:45

The first Adam was born both physically and spiritually alive, but he died spiritually when he sinned. The last Adam, Jesus, was also born physically and spiritually alive, but unlike the first Adam, Jesus never sinned, even though He was tempted in every way (Hebrews 4:15). God promised that redemption would come through the seed of a woman (Genesis 3:15; 17:19; Galatians 3:16). "Therefore the Lord himself will give you a sign. Behold, the virgin shall conceive and bear a son, and shall call his name Immanuel" (Isaiah 7:14). Jesus was one person with two natures. Our Kinsman Redeemer was fully God while also fully human.

Scripture makes the doctrine of the Incarnation a test of orthodoxy. "By this you know the Spirit of God: every spirit that confesses that Jesus Christ has come in the flesh is from God, and every spirit that does not confess Jesus is not from God. This is the spirit of the antichrist, which you heard was coming and now is in the world already" (1 John 4:2-3). Cults think Jesus was a good man. Spiritists think He was a psychic. Satan knows who Jesus is and "has blinded the minds of the unbelievers, to keep them from seeing the light of the gospel of the glory of Christ, who is the image of God" (2 Corinthians 4:4).

My response to God is:

_____

_____

_____

_____

THE DEITY OF CHRIST

Do nothing from rivalry or conceit, but in humility count others
more significant than yourselves. Let each of you look not only
to his own interests, but also to the interests of others. Have
this mind among yourselves, which is yours in Christ Jesus.

PHILIPPIANS 2:3-5

The humility of Jesus is the sternest possible rebuke to human pride. For us to become a worm to save worms doesn't remotely compare to Jesus, "who emptied himself, by taking the form [*morphe*] of a servant, being born in the likeness of men" (Philippians 2:7). *Morphe* stresses the inner essence or reality of that with which it is associated. Though Jesus "was in the form [*morphe*] of God, [He] did not count equality with God a thing to be grasped" (verse 6). Jesus didn't strive to be God because He was and is God. He was in essence both man and God.

Jesus stepped out of eternity into time so we can step out of time into eternity. He not only came to give us life; He *is* our life (Colossians 3:4). He left us an example to follow in His steps, of which the hardest is considering another person of less stature more important than ourselves. Self-interest rules this world, and the crucifixion is the sternest possible rebuke to human selfishness. Without the love of God, we would have never known the truth. Without the truth, we would never have known the love of God.

My response to God is:

_____

_____

_____

_____

_____

THE HOLY SPIRIT

"If anyone thirsts, let him come to me and drink. Whoever believes in me, as the Scripture has said, 'Out of his heart will flow rivers of living water.'" Now this he said about the Spirit, whom those who believed in him were to receive, for as yet the Spirit had not been given, because Jesus was not yet glorified.

JOHN 7:37-39

Joel prophesied the coming of the Holy Spirit at Pentecost (Joel 2:28-32; Acts 2:17-21), which happened when Jesus was exalted at the right hand of the Father (Acts 2:33). Pentecost was the beginning of the church age, when every believer is born again by a simple act of faith; baptized by the Holy Spirit into the body of Christ (1 Corinthians 12:13); indwelt perpetually by the Holy Spirit (Romans 8:38-39); and sealed by the Holy Spirit (Ephesians 1:13-14). When we are filled with the Holy Spirit, we sing a melody in our hearts to the Lord (5:19).

Jesus promised, "I will ask the Father, and he will give you another Helper, to be with you forever, even the Spirit of truth" (John 14:16-17). The Spirit of truth "will guide you into all the truth" (16:13), and that truth will set you free (8:32). The primary work of the Holy Spirit is to communicate God's presence to us. "The Spirit himself bears witness with our spirit that we are children of God" (Romans 8:16).

My response to God is:

_____

_____

_____

_____

_____

PRAYING BY THE SPIRIT

The Spirit helps us in our weakness. For we do not know what
to pray for as we ought, but the Spirit himself intercedes for
us with groanings too deep for words. And he who searches
hearts knows what is the mind of the Spirit, because the Spirit
intercedes for the saints according to the will of God.

ROMANS 8:26-27

We really don't know how or what to pray for, but the Holy Spirit does, and He helps us. The word *helps* in Greek is two prepositions before the word *take*. The Holy Spirit comes alongside, bears us up, and takes us across to the other side. Any prayer that God the Holy Spirit prompts us to pray is a prayer that God the Father is always going to answer. He not only helps us pray; He intercedes for us according to the will of God—and He is not the only member of the Trinity interceding for us. Jesus "is able to save to the uttermost those who draw near to God through him, since he always lives to make intercession for them" (Hebrews 7:25).

Knowing that we have two members of the Trinity praying for us is especially pertinent when confronting "the spiritual forces of evil in the heavenly places" (Ephesians 6:12). Paul defines our protective armor, and then he concludes by saying "praying at all times in the Spirit, with all prayer and supplication" (verse 18).

My response to God is:

_____

_____

_____

_____

_____

PRAYER AND THANKSGIVING

Let us come into his presence with thanksgiving; let us
make a joyful noise to him with songs of praise!

PSALM 95:2

There is only one way to approach God in prayer: with an attitude of gratitude. "The Lord is at hand; do not be anxious about anything, but in everything by prayer and supplication with thanksgiving let your requests be made known to God" (Philippians 4:6). "Continue steadfastly in prayer, being watchful in it with thanksgiving" (Colossians 4:2). "Rejoice always, pray without ceasing, give thanks in all circumstances; for this is the will of God in Christ Jesus for you" (1 Thessalonians 5:16-18).

Thank Him for giving us life, for forgiveness, for freedom, for meeting all our needs, for preparing a place for us in eternity. We glorify God by making ourselves known as Spirit-filled believers "giving thanks always and for everything to God the Father in the name of our Lord Jesus Christ" (Ephesians 5:20).

It would be good to follow Paul's example when we pray. "I do not cease to give thanks for you, remembering you in my prayers" (1:16). "I thank my God in all my remembrance of you, always in every prayer of mine for you" (Philippians 1:3-4). "We always thank God, the Father of our Lord Jesus Christ, when we pray for you" (Colossians 1:3). "We give thanks to God always for all of you, constantly mentioning you in our prayers" (1 Thessalonians 1:2).

My response to God is:

_____

_____

_____

_____

PRAYING FOR THE WAYWARD

How then will they call on him in whom they have not
believed? And how are they to believe in him of whom they
have never heard? And how are they to hear without someone
preaching? And how are they to preach unless they are sent?

ROMANS 10:14-15

When the Holy Spirit lays wayward people on our hearts, we can always pray for two things. First, "The harvest is plentiful, but the laborers are few. Therefore pray earnestly to the Lord of the harvest to send out laborers into his harvest" (Luke 10:2). God has chosen to work through believers in this church age to accomplish His purposes. Therefore, we should ask Him to send a messenger. When David wouldn't own up to his sin, God sent Nathan to confront him. (We may be someone's Nathan, since God has commissioned all of us to be His witnesses.)

Second, what Adam and Eve lost in the fall was life, and that is what Jesus came to give us. In the context of assurance for salvation (1 John 5:13) and assurance for answered prayer that is according to the will of God (verses 14-15), John wrote, "If anyone sees his brother committing a sin not leading to death, he shall ask, and God will give him life" (verse 16). So when God lays someone on your heart, ask Him to send that person a messenger and give life to that person.

My response to God is:

_____

_____

_____

_____

HEAR HIS VOICE

He is our God, and we are the people of his pasture, and the sheep of his hand. Today, if you hear his voice, do not harden your hearts.

PSALM 95:7-8

Often, quiet times with God aren't quiet. Our thoughts are distracted and even riddled with temptations directed at our vulnerabilities. We're hearing from everybody but God—or at least it seems that way. Maybe God is allowing that to get our attention, but in reality we are hearing from Him.

If you have a rebellious child who is always asking for one thing or another, what's on your mind, Mom or Dad? What would you like to talk to your child about? If any unresolved issues are between you and your heavenly Father, be assured that is what will be on your mind during quiet times. That is why the psalmist said, "Do not harden your hearts."

Nothing is more important than our relationship with God. He wants to remove the barriers that are keeping us from having an intimate relationship with Him. Rather than see an unresolved issue as a distraction, make it the subject of your prayer, which should lead to confession, repentance, and a new direction for life. Don't be deceived and think, *I can't talk to God about that.* He already knows about it, so why not be honest with Him? It just may set you free.

My response to God is:

_____

_____

_____

_____

_____

SILENCE

Be still, and know that I am God.

PSALM 46:10

A good way to assess the intimacy of our relationship with God is to get totally alone and see how well we tolerate solitude. Can we sit peacefully in His presence with a quiet mind and not feel obligated to say or do something? Silence is awkward when we're stuck someplace alone with a stranger. We feel almost obligated to say something. *The Yankees won again last night*, or *How do you like our weather?* On the other hand, a married couple who love each other can ride in a car together for hours and not feel obligated to say anything. They're comfortable in each other's presence.

Books are written about great saints who spent hours in prayer, and we wonder how they could do that. In all likelihood, much of that time was spent reading Scripture and listening. Intimate prayer with our heavenly Father may be more about listening than talking. Imagine a husband talking to his wife who sits there silently for an hour and then departs thinking they had a good conversation. If a church held an hour-long prayer service and spent the first 45 minutes listening, would the last 15 minutes be more productive than an hour of talking? Jesus said, "They will listen to my voice. So there will be one flock, one shepherd" (John 10:16) and "Everyone who is of the truth listens to my voice" (18:37).

My response to God is:

_____

_____

_____

_____

_____

HEART

Keep your heart with all vigilance, for from it flow the springs of life.

PROVERBS 4:23

H. Wheeler Robinson counted 822 uses of the word *heart* related to human personality.[1] Of those he found that 204 uses refer to the intellect, 195 uses are volitional, and 166 uses refer to an emotional state. Rather than think of the heart as the seat of emotion, it's more accurate to think of it as the seat of reflection. Moses said, "So teach us to number our days that we may get a heart of wisdom" (Psalm 90:12), and Proverbs 15:14 says, "The heart of him who has understanding seeks knowledge."

The heart is the center of self. Only in the heart do the mind, will, and emotions converge. Intellectual knowledge of a subject may not have any impact on our lives unless the truth enters our hearts. When it does, we are emotionally affected, and that drives the will. After reminding the people of Israel of all the ways God had provided for them, which they knew, Moses said, "But to this day the LORD has not given you a heart to understand or eyes to see or ears to hear" (Deuteronomy 29:4). David, a man after God's heart (1 Samuel 13:14) wrote, "Behold, you delight in truth in the inward being, and you teach me wisdom in the secret heart" (Psalm 51:6).

My response to God is:

_____

_____

_____

_____

_____

A HEART FOR GOD

Hear, O Israel: The LORD our God, the LORD is one. You
shall love the LORD your God with all your heart and
with all your soul and with all your might. And these
words I command you today shall be on your heart.

DEUTERONOMY 6:4-6

The above passage is referred to as the *Shema* (from the first word, *Hear*), which began Judaism's confession of faith. *Shema* meant to hear as though to obey. It was to be taught by the people to their children throughout the day. They were instructed to "bind them as a sign on your hand, and they shall be as frontlets between your eyes" (Deuteronomy 6:8). That probably referred to all that you think and do, but Orthodox Jews practiced this commandment by wearing phylacteries.

Thinking, feeling, and willing all come together in the heart in holistic unity. In the Bible, to "know" something is to grasp it such that it affects the total personality. For instance, "Adam knew Eve his wife, and she conceived and bore Cain" (Genesis 4:1). The heart is the place where God addresses us and from which we respond with all our hearts.

To make worship a holistic expression of the heart, the early church adopted practices that included all the senses—such as liturgy that is sung, incense, candles, bells, and icons that tell a biblical story. Such practices are still carried on by the Orthodox Church around the world, making worship a meaningful experience.

My response to God is:

_____

_____

_____

_____

_____

ARROGANCE

We know that "all of us possess knowledge." This "knowledge"
puffs up, but love builds up. If anyone imagines that he
knows something, he does not yet know as he ought to
know. But if anyone loves God, he is known by God.

1 CORINTHIANS 8:1-3

Where is the one who is wise? Where is the scribe? Where is the debater of this age? Has not God made foolish the wisdom of the world?" (1 Corinthians 1:20). From God's perspective, we have one eye just starting to slightly open: "Now we see in a mirror dimly, but then face to face" (13:12). One of the most crippling aspects of higher Christian education is academic arrogance. We can know theology and be arrogant, but we can't know God and be arrogant. In reality, the more we know, the more we realize how little we know.

We're confronted every day with the choice to either exalt ourselves or humble ourselves before Almighty God. Christian education will be maligned if we don't have the right goal. If we make knowledge an end in itself, we will distort the very purpose for which it was intended, which is to love God and others. Paul said those who have knowledge without love are a "noisy gong or a clanging cymbal" (verse 1). "By this all people will know that you are my disciples, if you have love for one another" (John 13:35).

My response to God is:

_____

_____

_____

_____

_____

TRAINING IN RIGHTEOUSNESS

All Scripture is breathed out by God and profitable for teaching, for reproof, for correction, and for training in righteousness, that the man of God may be complete, equipped for every good work.

2 TIMOTHY 3:16-17

God breathed into Adam, and he became a living being (Genesis 2:7). Scripture also comes alive by God's divine breath for those who are rightly related to Him, but the opposite is true for those who aren't. "They are darkened in their understanding, alienated from the life of God because of the ignorance that is in them, due to their hardness of heart" (Ephesians 4:18). If our pursuit of God is primarily academic, it leads to dead orthodoxy. In other words, it's theologically sound but spiritually dead.

"The one who looks into the perfect law, the law of liberty, and perseveres, being no hearer who forgets but a doer who acts, he will be blessed in his doing" (James 1:25). The first application we make upon reading God's Word is to us. Allow the Holy Spirit to bring conviction and then correction for you to be trained in righteousness. Academia wants to expand the mind, but God wants to enlarge the heart. "Search me, O God, and know my heart! Try me and know my thoughts! And see if there be any grievous way in me, and lead me in the way everlasting" (Psalm 139:23-24).

My response to God is:

_____

_____

_____

_____

_____

LIVING WORD

The word of God is living and active, sharper than any two-edged sword, piercing to the division of soul and spirit, of joints and of marrow, and discerning the thoughts and intentions of the heart. And no creature is hidden from his sight, but all are naked and exposed to the eyes of him to whom we must give account.

HEBREWS 4:12-13

The phrase "His sight" tells us this reference is not to the written word, Holy Scripture, but to the Word of God Himself, our Lord Jesus Christ. We also know this from the previous context, which is all about Jesus, who is greater than Moses and greater than angels.

Written words don't judge the thoughts and intentions of the heart. Only the living Word can do that. Jesus is the Word (John 1:14), and He is the Truth (14:6). Jesus said, "If you abide in my word, you are truly my disciples, and you will know the truth, and the truth will set you free" (8:31-32). Jesus is the Truth that sets us free. To abide in His word is to abide in Christ. "Whoever abides in me and I in him, he it is that bears much fruit, for apart from me you can do nothing" (15:5). Abide means to **a**lways **b**elieve in the **i**ndwelling **d**ivine **e**nergy. What makes Scripture come alive is the presence of God Himself, Who opens our eyes that we may see.

My response to God is:

_____

_____

_____

_____

_____

MENTAL STRONGHOLDS

Though we walk in the flesh, we are not waging war according to the flesh. For the weapons of our warfare are not of the flesh but have divine power to destroy strongholds.

2 CORINTHIANS 10:3-4

In this passage, Paul isn't talking about defensive armor. He's talking about the offensive weapons of God that tear down mental strongholds—flesh patterns that were erected in our minds before we came to Christ. They are mental habit patterns of thought burned into our minds over time. Essentially, they are assimilated from the environment in which we were raised in two primary ways.

The first is by the experiences we had growing up, such as the family we were raised in, the school we attended, the friends we had, and the church we went to or didn't go to. The second is traumatic experiences such as the divorce of parents, incest, or rape. People are not in bondage to past traumas but they may be in bondage to the lies they believe as a result of the trauma—lies such as *I'm not good. God doesn't love me. It's all my fault.* Such lies are often deeply embedded in our subconscious. Some of these flesh patterns are defense mechanisms, such as lying, denial, blaming, and rationalization.

God doesn't change our past; He sets us free from it. Jesus came to set captives free and heal the wounds of the brokenhearted. We are transformed by the renewing of our minds.

My response to God is:

_____

_____

_____

_____

_____

THE BATTLE FOR THE MIND

We destroy arguments and every lofty opinion raised against the knowledge of God, and take every thought captive to obey Christ.

2 CORINTHIANS 10:5

In the past we have made conscious choices and behaved accordingly. It takes about six weeks of routine behavior to establish a habit, which becomes a neural pathway in the brain. These mental habit patterns of thought have to be crucified and replaced by the truth. The brain is like the hardware in a computer system, whereas the mind is like the software. We can reprogram our minds, but we must be aware of "viruses," which are never accidental.

The devil will attempt to infiltrate our minds with his lies. The word *thought* in the above passage is the Greek word *noema*. It is seldom used in Scripture, but it occurs in 2 Corinthians, which is revealing. Paul urges us to forgive others "so that we would not be outwitted by Satan; for we are not ignorant of his designs [*noema*]" (2:11). "The god of this world has blinded the minds [*noema*] of the unbelievers, to keep them from seeing the light of the gospel" (4:4). "But I am afraid that as the serpent deceived Eve by his cunning, your thoughts [*noema*] will be led astray from a sincere and pure devotion to Christ" (11:3).

Satan's lies and worldly philosophies raised up against the knowledge of God are subjugated to Christ when we choose to believe the truth.

My response to God is:

_____

_____

_____

_____

_____

SATAN'S LIES

Then Satan stood against Israel and incited David to number Israel.

1 CHRONICLES 21:1

Satan will probably not come to someone like David, who had a whole heart for God, and entice him to sacrifice his babies. The deception would be too obvious. So what is wrong with taking a census? David wrote, "The king is not saved by his great army" (Psalm 33:16), and Joab knew it was a sin, but David did it anyway. Thousands died.

Satan wanted to shift David's confidence in God to his own resources. How did he do it? This was David's idea, or at least he thought it was, and therein lies the deception. Such thoughts come to us first-person singular, confusing us with our own thoughts. Satan infiltrated one of Jesus's disciples: "The devil had already put it into the heart of Judas Iscariot, Simon's son, to betray him" (John 13:2). Judas was a thief, and that's probably why he was vulnerable to Satan's lies. Ananias had sold his property and brought only a portion of the proceeds to the church, allowing others to think that was all he had. Peter asked, "Ananias, why has Satan filled your heart to lie to the Holy Spirit and to keep back for yourself part of the proceeds of the land?" (Acts 5:3). God striking Ananias and Sapphira dead was severe discipline, but it sent a clear message to the early church, warning them that Satan could control their behavior if they believed his lies.

My response to God is:

_____

_____

_____

_____

_____

VOICES

The Spirit clearly says that in later times some will abandon the faith and follow deceiving spirits and things taught by demons.

1 TIMOTHY 4:1 NIV

Evil acts of violence are randomly committed every day, and civil authorities are often puzzled by the motives for such acts. Often the perpetrator will confess to hearing "voices" telling them to commit such atrocities. Secular psychologists and psychiatrists work with people all the time who are struggling with tempting, condemning, and blasphemous thoughts. The world will interpret that as mental illness. Believing it to be a chemical imbalance, they prescribe antipsychotic medication. Likewise, people drink alcohol and take drugs because they have no mental peace. All that does is mask the symptoms. Remove the drug and the voices are back, so nothing is resolved.

How can our neurotransmitters in the brain randomly fire and create a thought that we are opposed to thinking? How can a chemical imbalance create a thought and a personality that often accompany the "voices" people hear? Evil is always personal, which is why the church has always believed in a personal devil. What Paul warned us about is presently happening all over the world, and it is likely the precursor to the coming apostasy, which will usher in the second coming of our Lord and Savior. Freeing people of demonic oppression was an evangelistic opportunity for the early church, and it will likely be the case in the end times.

My response to God is:

_____

_____

_____

_____

THE WORD IN OUR HEARTS

Let the peace of Christ rule in your hearts, to which
indeed you were called in one body. And be thankful.
Let the word of Christ dwell in you richly.

COLOSSIANS 3:15-16

Imagine your mind is a coffeepot, filled with dark, smelly coffee. One day you decide to clean up your mind, but you have no way to filter out the coffee. Then you notice a bowl of crystal-clear ice beside the coffeepot with a label that says, "The word of God." You can't pour the whole bowl in at once, but you can take one ice cube a day and fight off the temptation to put in another scoop of coffee.

Months later you can hardly smell, see, or taste the coffee that once filled the coffeepot. It's still there, but its influence is greatly diminished. However, there will be no progress if, as you put in one ice cube, you also put in one scoop of coffee (such as taking one peek at pornography or some other negative influence).

To rule literally means to act as an umpire, to arbitrate or decide. The peace of Christ should decide all matters of the heart for believers. "How can a young man keep his way pure? By guarding it according to your word. With my whole heart I seek you; let me not wander from your commandments! I have stored up your word in my heart, that I might not sin against you" (Psalm 119:9-11).

My response to God is:

_____

_____

_____

_____

_____

EMOTIONAL HONESTY

Having put away falsehood, let each one of you speak
the truth with his neighbor, for we are members one of
another. Be angry and do not sin; do not let the sun go down
on your anger, and give no opportunity to the devil.

EPHESIANS 4:25-27

Emotions are like an indicator light on the dash of a car. Covering up the irritating light with tape is suppression. Breaking the light with a hammer is indiscriminate expression. Looking under the hood is acknowledgment. Suppression is dishonest and unhealthful. We communicate verbally and nonverbally, and when they don't match, we believe the nonverbal.

It is a falsehood to say something incongruent with what we are actually feeling. The sin is not being angry; it's being dishonest about being angry but failing to "look under the hood." Being emotionally honest and speaking the truth in love makes for healthy relationships. Bottled up emotions are the basis for many psychosomatic illnesses. "When I kept silent [about my sin], my bones wasted away" (Psalm 32:3). Indiscriminate expression may be healthier for us, but potentially harmful to the other person. "Let every person be quick to hear, slow to speak, slow to anger; for the anger of man does not produce the righteousness of God" (James 1:19-20). Therefore, "confess [acknowledge/be honest about] your sins to one another and pray for one another, that you may be healed" (5:16).

My response to God is:

_____

_____

_____

_____

_____

MATURE THINKING

Brothers, do not be children in your thinking.
Be infants in evil, but in your thinking be mature.

1 CORINTHIANS 14:20

On Monday, a longtime employee finds a note from his boss on his desk asking him to come to his office on Friday at 10:00 a.m. The company has been downsizing, so he can't help but wonder why he's being summoned. At first he thinks he's going to be laid off after years of faithful service, and he becomes angry. Then thinks, *Maybe I'm not. But then again, maybe I am—or not*! Now he's anxious, because "he is a double-minded man, unstable in all his ways" (James 1:8). By Thursday he's convinced himself that he's going to be laid off, and he wonders how he can start over again at his age.

Now he's depressed, feeling hopeless and helpless. Friday comes, and he's an emotional wreck when he walks into the boss's office. "Congratulations," his boss says. "We've made you vice-president." Now how does he feel?

The anger, anxiety, and depression were all a product of his thoughts. If what we believe doesn't conform to truth, then what we feel doesn't conform to reality. People are doing what they are doing and feeling what they are feeling because of what they have chosen to think and believe. Therefore, we should be mature in what we think and certain of what we believe.

My response to God is:

_____

_____

_____

_____

_____

PAINFUL MEMORIES

Brothers, I do not consider that I have made it on my own.
But one thing I do: forgetting what lies behind and straining
forward to what lies ahead, I press on toward the goal for
the prize of the upward call of God in Christ Jesus.

PHILIPPIANS 3:13-14

Abused people struggle to make it on their own, but present events keep pushing their emotional buttons and their past keeps haunting them. There are places they can't go, people they can't see, and subjects they can't talk about because they trigger bad memories.

How does one forget what lies behind? We don't, at least not initially. But as new creations in Christ, we can reprocess what happened in the past from a different vantage point. We are not just a product of our past. We are a product of Christ's work on the cross. The lies we believed, because of the trauma, can be renounced and replaced with truth. We naturally try to suppress those damaged emotions, but God wants them to surface so we can let them go.

We do that by facing the truth, seeking forgiveness, and then forgiving those who have hurt us. Then we can do what God does, which is to remember our sins and other people's sins no more. The past no longer has any hold on us, and we are free to press on and be the people God called us to be.

My response to God is:

_____

_____

_____

_____

_____

PLANS

The heart of man plans his way, but the LORD establishes his steps.

PROVERBS 16:9

We plan our days, weeks, months, and years, but something almost always happens that interferes with those plans. We plan to be at work on time, but we're stuck in traffic, and we feel angry. We schedule a fund-raising event, but we're not sure how many people will come or if we will reach our goal, and we feel anxious. We want to succeed at work, but the promotion we wanted seems less and less likely, and that can be depressing. We become angry when our goals are blocked, anxious when meeting them is uncertain, and depressed when they seem impossible.

In an attempt to accomplish their goals, insecure people will seek to control other people and events when they have no right or ability to do so. Our goal might be to have a happy and harmonious family, yet every member of the family can block that goal. But nobody and nothing can keep us from being the spouse and parent God called us to be. Nobody can keep us from being the person God called us to be, and that is God's goal for our lives. The fruit of the Spirit is love and self-control, not child- and spouse-control. When our goal is love, then we have joy instead of depression, peace instead of anxiety, and patience instead of anger (see the fruit of the Spirit, Galatians 5:22-23).

My response to God is:

_____

_____

_____

_____

_____

ANGER

Whoever is slow to anger has great understanding,
but he who has a hasty temper exalts folly.

PROVERBS 14:29

Anger is the emotional response to what we are presently thinking, flesh patterns established in our past, and painful memories. Since emotions are a product of our thoughts, pay attention to what you're thinking when you leave the relatively controlled environment of your home and drive in heavily congested traffic. *Get off the phone! Who taught you to drive? Go! Go!* Anger is about control or the absence of it. Road rage is the reaction of those who can't control the traffic around them. Angry parenting is the inability to control our children. But those who are slow to anger have the mental discipline to be patient when life isn't going as they planned.

Angry flesh patterns develop early in life. Two-year-olds throw temper tantrums trying to get what they want. Bosses, coaches, and parents resort to outbursts of anger, causing their subjects to respond in fearful obedience. Smoldering anger motivates passive-aggressive people to manipulate those around them. As long as it gets the results they want, they will all keep doing it. God would see that as folly, which is a lack of good sense. Getting angry and being an angry person are two different issues. People who have suffered injustices can become bitterly angry and seek revenge unless they come to Christ, who will heal their wounds and set them free.

My response to God is:

_____

_____

_____

_____

RIGHTEOUS INDIGNATION

[Jesus] entered the temple and began to drive out those who sold
and those who bought in the temple, and he overturned the tables
of the money-changers and the seats of those who sold pigeons.

MARK 11:15

Righteous indignation is a justifiable reaction to the things that anger God, motivating us to confront injustices by taking appropriate action. Jesus was demonstrating this when He cleansed the temple. He was angry about the defamation of God's glory in His temple, and He did something about it.

If you want to get angry and not sin, then get angry the way Christ did. Get angry at sin. He turned over the tables, not the money changers. It takes courage to confront social injustices, but if the righteous don't take a stand they will continue. On another occasion Jesus entered a synagogue where there was a man with a withered hand. The Pharisees were watching to see if Jesus would heal him on the Sabbath. Jesus "said to them, 'Is it lawful on the Sabbath to do good or to do harm, to save life or to kill?' But they were silent. And he looked around at them with anger, grieved at their hardness of heart" (Mark 3:3-5).

Jesus was not responding to a blocked goal, because He has none. The wrath of God is part of His righteous nature. It will become part of our nature if we are growing in Christ.

My response to God is:

_____

_____

_____

_____

_____

REVENGE

ROMANS 12:18-19

Even if you perfectly loved everyone, there is no guarantee that they would love you back. Nor is it promised that you won't be victimized, but you don't have to remain a victim. *But I want justice and for the other person to suffer to the same degree I suffered.* Would that end your suffering? *But you don't know how bad they hurt me!* They are still hurting you. *But why should I let them off my hook?* That is precisely why you should—you're still hooked to them. But they're not off God's hook.

To forgive another is to set a captive free and to realize that you were the captive. What is to be gained is freedom from your past. *But where is the justice?* Justice is the cross. Jesus died for your sins and everyone else's. *I'll wait until I heal first; then maybe I'll forgive.* That will never happen, because you forgive so you will heal. Jesus came to set captives free and to heal the brokenhearted. In this world you will not have perfect justice, but God will make it right in the end. To err is human, but to forgive is divine.

My response to God is:

_____

_____

_____

_____

_____

FORGIVING OTHERS

Let all bitterness and wrath and anger and clamor and slander be
put away from you, along with all malice. Be kind to one another,
tenderhearted, forgiving one another, as God in Christ forgave you.

EPHESIANS 4:31-32

Christ forgave us by taking the consequences for our sins on Himself. When we forgive another person, we're agreeing to live with the consequences of that person's sin. *But that's not fair!* Of course it's not, but you will have to live with them anyway. Everyone is living with the consequences of somebody else's sin. The whole world is living with the consequences of Adam's sin. The only real choice is to do that in the bondage of bitterness or in the freedom of forgiveness. There has been enough pain; choose forgiveness. It's the most Christlike thing we can do.

We don't forgive others for their sake; we do it for the sake of our own freedom and our relationship with our heavenly Father. It's primarily an issue between ourselves and God, and we can forgive anytime, like right now. To forgive from the heart, we have to let God into our emotional core. Ask Him to reveal whom you need to forgive. As names come to mind, say, *Lord, I forgive* [name] *for* [specifically mention every hurtful thing that comes to mind and how it made you feel, such as worthless, rejected, unloved, dirty, embarrassed].

My response to God is:

_____

_____

_____

_____

_____

SEEKING FORGIVENESS

If you are offering your gift at the altar and there remember
that your brother has something against you, leave your
gift there before the altar and go. First be reconciled to
your brother, and then come and offer your gift.

MATTHEW 5:23-24

If someone has hurt you, don't go to them; go to God. You can't go to those who have died but you still need to forgive, and it's inadvisable to go to those who have abused you. It could lead to further abuse. However, if you have offended someone else, don't continue religious observances in hypocrisy when God has brought that person to your mind. Go to that person and seek their forgiveness, hoping for reconciliation, and pay for damages if called for.

Don't document it for legal reasons or send a letter or email unless that is the only way to communicate. Go in person and say, "Would you forgive me for [specifically say what you did without explanation or rationalization]." It's manipulative to do that hoping they will own up to the sins they have committed. Whether they forgive you or not is their choice. If they choose not to forgive you, you aren't obligated to do anything more—unless you need to pay for the damage that was done. Then go to church with a clear conscience. Paul said, "I always take pains to have a clear conscience toward both God and man" (Acts 24:16).

My response to God is:

_____

_____

_____

_____

_____

SINGLE VISION

The eye is the lamp of the body. So, if your eye is healthy,
your whole body will be full of light, but if your eye is
bad, your whole body will be full of darkness. If then the
light in you is darkness, how great is the darkness!

MATTHEW 6:22-23

Ancient tradition viewed the eyes as the windows through which light entered the body. If the eyes were in good condition, the whole body received the benefits that light bestows. But if there was something wrong with the eyes, the whole body was plunged into the darkness, which breeds disease.

A subtle nuance in this passage is pregnant with meaning. The "clear eye" is the one with a single vision, which Jesus clarifies in the next verse: "No one can serve two masters, for either he will hate the one and love the other, or he will be devoted to the one and despise the other. You cannot serve God and money" (Matthew 6:24). There will be no peace serving two masters. "For the love of money [not money itself] is a root of all kinds of evils. It is through this craving that some have wandered away from the faith and pierced themselves with many pangs" (1 Timothy 6:10). We choose which master we will serve—God or the riches of this world. Whichever master we choose, by that master we shall be controlled.

My response to God is:

_____

_____

_____

_____

_____

DENYING SELF

If anyone would come after me, let him deny himself
and take up his cross daily and follow me.

LUKE 9:23

Denying ourselves is not the same as self-denial. Athletes, politicians, and publicity seekers deny themselves certain pleasures to win or to promote themselves. Self is still the dominate force. Denying self is abdicating self-rule. God never designed our souls to function as masters. Self-seeking, self-serving, self-justifying, self-glorifying, self-centered, and self-confident living is in actuality serving the world, the flesh, and the devil.

We have to die to ourselves to live in Christ. We are forgiven because He died in our place. We are delivered because we have died with Him. "I have been crucified with Christ; and it is no longer I who live, but Christ lives in me; and the life which I now live in the flesh I live by faith in the Son of God, who loved me and gave Himself up for me" (Galatians 2:20 NASB). If we hold on to our natural identity and earthly inheritance, we rob ourselves of an infinitely better spiritual identity and an eternal inheritance. Jesus said, "Follow Me." Self will never cast out self; we have to be led into it by the Holy Spirit. "We who live are constantly being delivered over to death for Jesus' sake, that the life of Jesus also may be manifested in our mortal flesh" (2 Corinthians 4:11 NASB).

My response to God is:

_____

_____

_____

_____

_____

SOME SACRIFICE!

Whoever would save his life will lose it, but whoever loses
his life for my sake will save it. For what does it profit a man
if he gains the whole world and loses or forfeits himself?

LUKE 9:24-25

The repudiation of our natural life may seem austere, but what are we actually sacrificing? First, we sacrifice the pleasure of things to gain the pleasures of life. What would we exchange for the fruit of the Spirit? A new car? A better house? Social status?

Second, we sacrifice the lower life to gain the higher life. If we aim for this world, we miss the next, but if we aim for the next world, we get heaven and the blessings of knowing God now. "Train yourself for godliness; for while bodily training is of some value, godliness is of value in every way, as it holds promise for the present life and also for the life to come" (1 Timothy 4:7-8).

Third, we sacrifice the temporal to gain the eternal. Missionary Jim Elliot said, "He is no fool who gives what he cannot keep to gain what he cannot lose."

"Godliness with contentment is great gain, for we brought nothing into the world, and we cannot take anything out of the world. But if we have food and clothing, with these we will be content" (6:6-8). Contentment itself is a blessing from God.

My response to God is:

_____

_____

_____

_____

_____

SELF-INTEREST

Peter took [Jesus] aside and began to rebuke him, saying, "Far be it from you, Lord! This shall never happen to you." But he turned and said to Peter, "Get behind me, Satan! You are a hindrance to me. For you are not setting your mind on the things of God, but on the things of man."

MATTHEW 16:22-23

This memorable rebuke seems mercilessly severe, yet the crediting of Satan as the source describes exactly and appropriately the character of the advice given by Peter. *Save yourself at any rate. Sacrifice duty to self-interest, the cause of Christ to personal convenience.* This advice is truly satanic in principle, for the whole aim of Satan is to get self-interest recognized as the chief end of man.

Satan is called the "prince of this world" because self-interest rules this fallen world. Satan doesn't believe that even the sons of God have a higher motive: *Does Job or even Jesus serve God for nothing? Self-sacrifice, suffering for righteousness's sake, commitment to truth even unto death: It is pure romance and youthful sentimentalism or at best hypocritical. There is no such thing as surrender of the lower life for the higher life; all men are selfish at heart and have their price. Some may hold out longer than others, but in the end every man will prefer his own things to the things of God.*

Such is Satan's creed. We find ourselves through the mystery of self-sacrifice.

My response to God is:

_____

_____

_____

_____

_____

PRIMORDIAL FEAR

The LORD God called to [Adam] and said to him, "Where are
you?" And he said, "I heard the sound of you in the garden,
and I was afraid, because I was naked, and I hid myself."

GENESIS 3:9-10

The immediate emotional consequence of being separated from God was fear. Why was Adam afraid? There was nothing in the Garden of Eden to be afraid of. He had no neurological illness that needed medication. He had no learned phobias that had to be unlearned or flesh patterns that had to be crucified. But separated from God, Adam felt the terror of being utterly alone, abandoned, exposed, and vulnerable.

Throughout history, people have been afraid of the idea of impermanence. They have taken extreme measures to overcome their mortality. Fanciful beliefs have been formulated by false religions to give them hope for an afterlife. Explorers have searched for the mystical Fountain of Youth. This primordial fear exists in all humanity, and there is only one antidote. Jesus came to give us eternal life, which is not the same as temporal life that defines our physical existence. "Since the children share in flesh and blood, He Himself likewise also partook of the same, so that through death He might render powerless him who had the power of death, that is, the devil, and might free those who through fear of death were subject to slavery all their lives" (Hebrews 2:14-15 NASB).

My response to God is:

_____

_____

_____

_____

_____

FEAR OF GOD

Do not call conspiracy all that this people calls conspiracy, and
do not fear what they fear, nor be in dread. But the LORD of
hosts, him you shall honor as holy. Let him be your fear, and
let him be your dread. And he will become a sanctuary.

ISAIAH 8:12-14

Fear is the most basic of all natural instincts, and we're afraid when we sense our physical or psychological safety is threatened. Fear always has an object, and for it to be threatening it must be perceived as both imminent and potent. We don't fear poisonous snakes when none are present, and we don't fear them when they are dead. Remove one of the attributes, and the object is no longer feared.

God is the ultimate fear object because He is omnipresent and omnipotent. That is why "the fear of the LORD is the beginning of wisdom; all those who practice it have a good understanding" (Psalm 111:10). The fear of God is the one fear that can expel all other fears. "There is no fear in love, but perfect love casts out fear. For fear has to do with punishment, and whoever fears has not been perfected in love" (1 John 4:18). The punishment we deserved has fallen on Christ. However, we live to please God, because we will appear before Him and give an account for everything we have done. "Therefore, knowing the fear of the Lord, we persuade others" (2 Corinthians 5:11).

My response to God is:

_____

_____

_____

_____

_____

FEAR OF DEATH

Death is swallowed up in victory. O death, where is
your victory? O death, where is your sting?

1 CORINTHIANS 15:54-55

It is appointed for man to die once, and after that comes judgment" (Hebrews 9:27). Physical death is imminent, but it is no longer potent. Paul said, "For me to live is Christ, and to die is gain" (Philippians 1:21). Nothing else fits the formula. But for me to live is my job, family, friends, vacation, and so on, and to die is loss.

"So we are always of good courage. We know that while we are at home in the body we are away from the Lord, for we walk by faith, not by sight. Yes, we are of good courage, and we would rather be away from the body and at home with the Lord" (2 Corinthians 5:6-8). Knowing this is not a license to commit suicide. We are required to be good stewards of the life God has entrusted to us. Those who are free from the fear of death are free to live and boldly face life's challenges as Paul did: "We do not want you to be unaware, brothers, of the affliction we experienced in Asia. For we were so utterly burdened beyond our strength that we despaired of life itself. Indeed, we felt that we had received the sentence of death. But that was to make us rely not on ourselves but on God who raises the dead" (1:8-9).

My response to God is:

_____

_____

_____

_____

_____

FEAR OF MAN

Do not fear those who kill the body but cannot kill the soul.
Rather fear him who can destroy both soul and body in hell.

MATTHEW 10:28

Fear is a powerful motivator, and fearing people more than we fear God is mutually exclusive to faith in God. People will always be present as long as we are alive on planet Earth, so what power do they have over us? Only what we give them. That is not a license to be rebellious against governing authorities, but there may be times when we must obey God rather than man. The apostles were brought before the council and told, "We strictly charged you not to teach in this name, yet here you have filled Jerusalem with your teaching" (Acts 5:28). Peter responded, "We must obey God rather than men" (verse 29).

"Now who is there to harm you if you are zealous for what is good? But even if you should suffer for righteousness' sake, you will be blessed. Have no fear of them, nor be troubled, but in your hearts honor Christ the Lord as holy, always being prepared to make a defense to anyone who asks you for a reason for the hope that is in you; yet do it with gentleness and respect, having a good conscience, so that, when you are slandered, those who revile your good behavior in Christ may be put to shame" (1 Peter 3:13-16).

My response to God is:

_____

_____

_____

_____

_____

FEAR OF SATAN

Be sober-minded; be watchful. Your adversary the devil prowls
around like a roaring lion, seeking someone to devour. Resist him,
firm in your faith, knowing that the same kinds of suffering are
being experienced by your brotherhood throughout the world.

1 PETER 5:8-9

Most people would be paralyzed in fear if they heard a lion roar. For Satan, it's a scare tactic that gets people to respond in fear rather than in faith, and it works. Far more people fear Satan than fear God, and that is even true in churches. The fact that people throughout the world are experiencing his ruthless tactics means that encountering our adversary is imminent. But he is no longer potent. God "disarmed the rulers and authorities and put them to open shame, by triumphing over them in him" (Colossians 2:15).

"We know that we are children of God, and that the whole world is under the control of the evil one" (1 John 5:19 NIV). The kingdom of darkness is ruled by lies and intimidation. Satan wants to be feared because he wants to be worshipped as the god of this world. The moment we fear Satan more than we fear God, we elevate him as a greater object of worship. "We know that everyone who has been born of God does not keep on sinning, but [Christ] who was born of God protects him, and the evil one does not touch him" (verse 18).

My response to God is:

_____

_____

_____

_____

_____

NIGHT TERROR

Now a word was brought stealthily; my ear received the whisper of it. Amid thoughts from visions of the night, when deep sleep falls on men, dread came upon me, and trembling, which made all my bones shake. A spirit glided past my face; the hair of my flesh stood up. It stood still, but I could not discern its appearance. A form was before my eyes; there was silence, then I heard a voice: "Can mortal man be in the right before God? Can a man be pure before his Maker?"

JOB 4:12-17

That was a visitation from the "accuser of our brethren" (Revelation 12:10 NASB), not God. People all over the world are having similar nighttime terror attacks. It often feels like a pressure on the chest or throat accompanied by a fear that makes our hair stand up. It can feel like we're pinned to the bed and unable to speak, which is an attempt to keep us from calling on the name of the Lord and being saved (Acts 2:21). Remember, "the weapons of our warfare are not of the flesh" (2 Corinthians 10:4).

We stop the attack by first submitting to God and then resisting the devil, who will flee from us (James 4:7). We can submit to God inwardly because He knows the thoughts and intentions of our hearts. The moment we call on God, we can verbally resist the devil. All we have to say is, "Jesus."

My response to God is:

_____

_____

_____

_____

_____

PHOBIAS

I sought the LORD, and he answered me
and delivered me from all my fears.

PSALM 34:4

The most repeated commandment in Scripture is "Fear not," but saying that to someone with a phobia falls on deaf ears. Phobias are irrational fears rooted in a lie. To overcome them, we start by asking God to reveal to our mind the lie behind the phobia. Valuable insight comes from knowing when we first experienced that fear and what events preceded that experience. God will lead us back to that event and show us the root of our phobia if we sincerely ask Him.

God confronted Saul through Samuel's revealing that he feared the voice of the people more than the voice of God (1 Samuel 15:24). We need to know the truth to be set free. In what way is the fear object imminent or potent? Which attribute can be overcome? How has any phobia prevented us from living responsibly or motivated us to live irresponsibly? Once we have analyzed our fear, we can work out a plan of responsible behavior.

Do the thing we fear the most, and the death of fear is certain. This may require baby steps at first, so we can't set ourselves up for failure. We should determine in advance what our reaction will be when confronted with any fear object. Finally, we must commit ourselves to carry out the plan. The key to any cure is commitment.

My response to God is:

_____

_____

_____

_____

_____

DEPRESSION

How long, O LORD? Will you forget me forever? How long
will you hide your face from me? How long must I take
counsel in my soul and have sorrow in my heart all the
day? How long shall my enemy be exalted over me?

PSALM 13:1-2

Depression has been called the common cold of mental illness. When experiencing the "blues," we feel hopeless and helpless in the midst of our circumstances, and such was the case for David in Psalm 13. In Psalm 38, David expresses almost every symptom of depression (poor health—verse 3, despair—verse 4, mourning—verse 6, feebleness—verse 8, low energy—verse 10, being isolated and withdrawn—verse 11, negative thoughts—verse 12). God sought out David because he was "a man after his own heart" (1 Samuel 13:14).

In Psalm 13, however, David is depressed for one major reason: He thinks God has forgotten him forever. God couldn't forget anyone even for a moment much less forever. But if that is what we believe, then we feel helpless and hopeless. David overcomes depression by first recalling, "I have trusted in your steadfast love" (verse 5). Then he expresses hope: "My heart shall rejoice in your salvation" (verse 5). Finally, he exercises his will: "I will sing to the LORD" (verse 6).

Martin Luther, like David, had numerous bouts with depression, and like David, he turned to music to overcome his sorrow. We are the benefactors. He wrote "A Mighty Fortress Is Our God."

My response to God is:

_____

_____

_____

_____

_____

HOPELESSNESS

He has made my teeth grind on gravel, and made me cower in ashes; my soul is bereft of peace; I have forgotten what happiness is; so I say, "My endurance has perished; so has my hope from the LORD."

LAMENTATIONS 3:16-18

Jeremiah has been called the "weeping prophet," and he's the likely author of Lamentations. In chapter 3, he believes God is the cause of his afflictions, and he feels bitter and depressed. He believes God is the source of his problems and that He "walled" him in. Jeremiah was mired in depression and ready to call it quits until he thought, "But this I call to mind, and therefore I have hope: The steadfast love of the LORD never ceases; his mercies never come to an end; they are new every morning; great is your faithfulness. 'The LORD is my portion,' says my soul, 'therefore I will hope in him'" (verses 21-24).

Nothing had changed in his circumstances. What changed was what he believed. It was like our taking a time-limited exam and feeling hopeless as the minutes pass because we can't recall the information we need, but then suddenly it comes to our mind and hope returns. This is why we worship God, keeping His divine attributes fresh in our memory. The psalmist asked, "Why are you cast down, O my soul, and why are you in turmoil within me? Hope in God; for I shall again praise him, my salvation and my God" (Psalm 42:11).

My response to God is:

_____

_____

_____

_____

_____

HELPLESSNESS

"I will bring you into the land that I swore to give to Abraham, to Isaac, and to Jacob. I will give it to you for a possession. I am the LORD." Moses spoke thus to the people of Israel, but they did not listen to Moses, because of their broken spirit and harsh slavery.

EXODUS 6:8-9

Adult elephants staked to the ground can pop out the stake in an instant, but they don't because they couldn't when they were infants. Learned helplessness keeps humans and animals enslaved. Hundreds of years of slavery were deeply embedded in the minds of the Jewish people. God promised to deliver them from Egypt, but they wouldn't even listen to Moses. Ten of the 12 spies gave a negative report of the Promised Land, and that discouraged the people, who then rebelled against Moses (Numbers 14). There will always be blessing snatchers who see only the risks.

It's depressing to believe that we *can't* when we *can* do all things through Christ who strengthens us (Philippians 4:13). Both doubters and believers are faced with trials and tribulations, but the faithful believe the promises of God and have a vision for what can be gained by trusting Him. It takes no more energy to believe we can than it does to believe we can't. "Let us then with confidence draw near to the throne of grace, that we may receive mercy and find grace to help in time of need" (Hebrews 4:16).

My response to God is:

_____

_____

_____

_____

_____

POST ADRENAL EXHAUSTION

> Ahab told Jezebel all that Elijah had done, and how he had killed all the prophets with the sword. Then Jezebel sent a messenger to Elijah, saying, "So may the gods do to me and more also, if I do not make your life as the life of one of them by this time tomorrow."

1 KINGS 19:1-2

Elijah had just slain 450 prophets of Baal when he prayed for rain to end a drought, and it came. He told Ahab to prepare his chariot lest the rain stop him from going to Jezreel, and then he outran him on foot to the entrance to the city (1 Kings 18:46).

Great victories can be followed by great defeats if we're not careful. When we feel super-energized and burn the candle at both ends for an extended period of time, we will likely crash. That is post adrenal exhaustion, and it leaves us vulnerable to the enemy.

Jezebel cursed Elijah, this mighty man of God. "Then he was afraid, and he arose and ran for his life" (19:3). He believed a lie. He didn't die the next day, but he wanted to (verse 4). Curses made to our face are ineffective unless we believe them. Elijah was exhausted and lay down under a broom tree and slept. Then "an angel touched him and said to him, 'Arise and eat'" (verse 5). God meets us where we are. Food and rest are what we need when our adrenal glands are exhausted.

My response to God is:

_____

_____

_____

_____

_____

DEPRESSION TRIAD

May the God of hope fill you with all joy and peace in believing, so
that by the power of the Holy Spirit you may abound in hope.

ROMANS 15:13

Counselors have observed that depressed people have a negative view of themselves, their present circumstances, and the future. The Holy Spirit lifts us above this trio of negative thinking. The spiritual fruit of joy and peace are the antithesis of depression, and hope is the present assurance of some future good. "The Spirit himself bears witness with our spirit that we are children of God" (Romans 8:16).

No earthly position or name that we could make for ourselves remotely compares to the identity and position we have in Christ. Liberated children of God don't have a negative view of themselves nor an inflated one. The Holy Spirit will guide us into the future and has the power to accomplish God's sovereign will. The will of God will never take us where the grace of God cannot keep us. Present circumstances don't determine who we are, nor can they prevent God from meeting all our needs according to His riches in glory (Philippians 4:19). Our role is to believe that we can do all things through Christ who strengthens us (verse 13). Knowing that and being filled with the Holy Spirit is what enabled Paul to say, "I have learned in whatever situation I am to be content" (verse 11).

My response to God is:

_____

_____

_____

_____

_____

LOSSES

Whatever gain I had, I counted as loss for the sake of Christ. Indeed, I count everything as loss because of the surpassing worth of knowing Christ Jesus my Lord. For his sake I have suffered the loss of all things and count them as rubbish, in order that I may gain Christ.

PHILIPPIANS 3:7-8

Reaction to losses in our lives is the primary cause for depression. The loss doesn't even have to be real. Imagined and threatened losses can have the same emotional response if we believe them. Christians aren't immune from suffering losses, because someday we shall lose everything we now possess. We suffer, too, but we don't have to "grieve as others do who have no hope" (1 Thessalonians 4:13).

Losses can be concrete, such as the loss of a job, our health, a spouse, or a house. Abstract losses are harder to identify and sometimes harder to overcome. Paul lost everything he had when God struck him down. He lost all his Jewish friends, his reputation, his social status, and his self-respect, and he had to live with the fact that he was the chief of all sinners, having zealously persecuted the church. After his conversion, he went away for three years. Undoubtedly, this was to renew his mind, but it's safe to assume that this was also a time to grieve over his losses, overcome his disappointments, and rebuild a shattered perception of himself.

But look what he gained.

My response to God is:

_____

_____

_____

_____

_____

REACTION TO LOSSES

So we do not lose heart. Though our outer nature is
wasting away, our inner nature is being renewed day by
day. For this slight momentary affliction is preparing for
us an eternal weight of glory beyond all comparison.

2 CORINTHIANS 4:16-17

We live and make plans as though tomorrow will be like today, and then unexpectedly we experience a crisis or loss that alters our course of life and disrupts our lifestyle. God doesn't allow such times to destroy us but to reveal who we are. The initial reaction is often denial, which can last for a minute or all our lives.

Many will wonder, *How can this be happening to me?*, which is often followed by the angry response *Why me?* Some try to reverse the loss by bargaining with God and others, but when that doesn't work, they feel hopeless and depressed. From there they either resign and drop out or accept what's happened as part of living in this fallen world.

We can't change what happened, but we can change who we are and come through the crisis a better person. Buzz Aldrin, the second man to walk on the moon, said, "My depression forced me, at the age of forty-one, to stop and, for the first time, examine my life."[2]

My response to God is:

_____

_____

_____

_____

_____

MENTAL CONSTRUCTS

One thing I do: forgetting what lies behind and straining
forward to what lies ahead, I press on toward the goal for
the prize of the upward call of God in Christ Jesus.

PHILIPPIANS 3:13-14

It took some time for Paul to bounce back after his losses, but some people never recover. Three mental constructs determine how long it will take, if ever, to recover from tragedies. The first is whether we think the consequences have a short- or long-term effect on us. Depression will be prolonged if we believe a loss will have a negative impact for the rest of our lives.

The second is how pervasive we believe the negative consequences are. If we believe they will ruin our whole lives, they just may. We grieve over losses, but a prolonged depression signifies an overattachment to people, places, and things that we have no right or ability to control.

The third is when we overly personalize the crisis and believe it's all our fault.

To overcome our losses, we need to change how we think from "I'm the problem" to "It's a problem." From "In everything" to "In this one thing." From "Forever" to "For a season." Someone said, "The bend in the road is not the end of the road, unless we fail to make the turn." Paul made the turn and then pressed on to become a model of perseverance and devotion to Christ.

My response to God is:

_____

_____

_____

_____

_____

WALKING IN DARKNESS

Who among you fears the Lord and obeys the voice of his servant?
Let him who walks in darkness and has no light trust in the name
of the Lord and rely on his God. Behold, all you who kindle a
fire, who equip yourselves with burning torches! Walk by the
light of your fire, and by the torches that you have kindled! This
you will have from my hand; you shall lie down in torment.

ISAIAH 50:10-11

Isaiah is referring to the darkness of uncertainty, not the darkness of sin. Such times seem like God has suspended His conscious blessings, and every natural instinct tells us to stop. But Scripture says to keep on walking in the light of previous revelation. Never doubt in darkness what God has shown us in the light.

The temptation is to create our own light. God allows it, but misery follows. God promised Abraham that his descendants would be as numerous as the stars, and then God turned out the light. Years went by, and Sarah was beyond the means of normal childbirth. So Abraham created his own light. Sarah supplied the match and offered her handmaiden, Hagar, and the whole world now suffers in torment (Arab and Jew). God called Moses to set His people free, but Moses tried it his way with a sword. Forty years later, God turned the light back on in a bush.

No matter how dark the night, morning comes.

My response to God is:

_____

_____

_____

_____

_____

STRESS

Preparing your minds for action, and being sober-
minded, set your hope fully on the grace that will be
brought to you at the revelation of Jesus Christ.

1 PETER 1:13

Our adrenal glands respond when we're under a certain amount of
stress by secreting cortisol (a natural hormone) into our blood-
stream. This is a natural flight or fight response to the pressures of life.
When stress persists too long, it becomes distress, the system breaks
down, and we become physically sick. Stress is a major cause of heart
disease and cancer.

However, when two people of equal stature are subjected to the
same environment, one can flourish while the other doesn't. The difference is how they perceive the environment—in other words, what
they believe about what they're experiencing. We are not shaped by
our environment; we are shaped by how we perceive it. Our five senses
bring data to the brain, but the mind interprets it. That is what determines the signal sent to our adrenal glands.

We have no control of our glands, which are part of the autonomic nervous system, but we do have control of what we think and
believe. Rather than being controlled by outside circumstances, believers should be directed from within. Jesus was never stressed out, and
we have the same potential if we are sober-minded, because "we have
the mind of Christ" (1 Corinthians 2:16). Wisdom is seeing life from
God's perspective.

My response to God is:

_____

_____

_____

_____

THE DIVINE PREREQUISITE

If anyone's will is to do God's will, he will know whether the teaching
is from God or whether I am speaking on my own authority.

JOHN 7:17

The one essential prerequisite to knowing God's will is for our will to be in line with His even before we know what it is. Suppose a closed door has a sign on it that says, "On the other side of this door is God's will for your life." We wonder, *What is it?* Why are we asking? So we can decide whether we want to go through the door?

If we want to fulfill our calling in Christ, we have to decide something on this side of the door. If God is God, then He has the right to decide what's on the other side of the door for us. And if we don't give Him that right, then we're acting as our own god. By faith we step through that door believing that God's will "is good and acceptable and perfect" (Romans 12:2).

There is no better place to be than in the center of God's will, no matter where it takes us. Progress is stalled if we stick our foot in the door, keeping it open in case we want to go back. Jesus said, "No one who puts his hand to the plow and looks back is fit for the kingdom of God" (Luke 9:62).

My response to God is:

_____

_____

_____

_____

_____

THE DOOR

Truly, truly, I say to you, I am the door of the
sheep. All who came before me are thieves and
robbers, but the sheep did not listen to them.

JOHN 10:7-8

Imagine stepping through "the door" into a narrow street with buildings on both sides, and in the distance you see Jesus beckoning you to come to Him. At the same time, voices are coming from the buildings: merchants tempting you, prostitutes enticing you, and philosophers pointing out the absurdity of following Jesus.

Mentally bombarded by temptations, accusations, insults, and lies, one man gives in, sits down, and makes no progress toward Jesus. A second man fights back: *That's not true. I'm not going in there. You can't make me. God does love me.* It may appear he is fighting the good fight, but actually the devil is setting the agenda, and progress is stalled. A third man tries not to entertain the negative thoughts bombarding his mind, but with little success.

Many distractors are on the path toward Jesus, but no insurmountable obstacles. Scripture doesn't instruct us to stop thinking negative thoughts, but we are encouraged to think about that which is true, honorable, just, pure, lovely, and commendable (Philippians 4:8). We're not called to dispel the darkness; we're called to turn on the light.

A fourth man doesn't pay attention to distracting thoughts. Instead, he chooses to believe the truth and live accordingly by faith, and more and more the noise lessens.

My response to God is:

_____

_____

_____

_____

THE NARROW WAY

Enter by the narrow gate. For the gate is wide and the way
is easy that leads to destruction, and those who enter by
it are many. For the gate is narrow and the way is hard
that leads to life, and those who find it are few.

MATTHEW 7:13-14

Suppose you're on a narrow road winding up a mountain. On the right is a cliff, and on the left is a roaring forest fire. Behind you is a deceiving serpent, and ahead of you is a sanctuary. As you're trudging up the slope, you realize a tempting option is on the right. Just sail off the cliff and enjoy the exhilaration of the free fall, even though that choice has a serious consequence—the sudden stop at the end. That is the nature of temptation; it looks good and may be fun…for a while.

On the left are the threatening flames—the flames of hell—ready to claim you if you stray off the path or fail to endure to the end. The serpent hisses, *Come on and jump. Everyone is doing it. You know you want to. Who would know?* So you jump, and the serpent changes roles from tempter to accuser: *You did it now. You're a failure. There's no hope for you, you sicko!*

The narrow way is neither license nor legalism, but freedom. "Now the Lord is the Spirit, and where the Spirit of the Lord is, there is freedom" (2 Corinthians 3:17).

My response to God is:

_____

_____

_____

_____

_____

GUIDING SHEEP

Then he led out his people like sheep and guided
them in the wilderness like a flock. He led them
in safety, so that they were not afraid.

PSALM 78:52-53

Shepherds have many tasks tending to their flocks, and one is to protect them from themselves. When left alone in moist green pastures, sheep will literally eat until they bloat and die. The psalmist wrote, "The LORD is my shepherd; I shall not want. He makes me lie down in green pastures" (Psalm 23:1-2). We can have too much of a good thing.

Australian sheep dogs are trained to keep the flock moving by chasing them from the rear and the flanks. The shepherds of Israel, however, led from the front. When it was time to move the sheep, the shepherd would stand up and say something, and then all the sheep would look up and follow him. Jesus said, "My sheep hear my voice, and I know them, and they follow me. I give them eternal life, and they will never perish, and no one will snatch them out of my hand. My Father, who has given them to me, is greater than all, and no one is able to snatch them out of the Father's hand" (John 10:27-29).

God has a grip on and won't let go of those who follow Him. He will protect us from the evil one and from ourselves when we're tempted to overindulge or stray.

My response to God is:

_____

_____

_____

_____

_____

SPIRITUAL GUIDANCE

The Helper, the Holy Spirit, whom the Father will send in my name, he will teach you all things and bring to your remembrance all that I have said to you...he will guide you into all the truth.

JOHN 14:26; 16:13

A young pilot had just passed the written exam for instrument landing, and this was his first experience actually doing it. With zero visibility, he radioed the control tower asking for permission to land. The air traffic controller said he would have to be placed in a holding pattern and wait for further instructions. The slightly nervous pilot informed the controller that this was his first attempt at instrument landing and he could use a little assistance. "You got it," the controller said. "Just remember the instructions in the flight manual that got you to where you are."

The pilot began rehearsing in his mind all he learned in aviation school as the controller kept adjusting his flight pattern. It dawned on him that he was putting all his trust in a person he couldn't see, who was guiding him around obstacles he couldn't see and helping him to avoid collisions with other aircraft. Finally, instructions came to make the landing, which he safely did.

The Holy Spirit brings to our mind the Word of God and guides us through the maze of life. "For all who are led by the Spirit of God are sons of God" (Romans 8:14).

My response to God is:

_____

_____

_____

_____

_____

DIVINE GUIDANCE

They went through the region of Phrygia and Galatia, having been
forbidden by the Holy Spirit to speak the word in Asia. And when they
had come up to Mysia, they attempted to go into Bithynia, but the
Spirit of Jesus did not allow them... And a vision appeared to Paul in
the night: a man of Macedonia... saying, "Come over to Macedonia."

ACTS 16:6-9

If God wanted Paul to go to Macedonia from Jerusalem, it would have been easier to catch a boat in Caesarea. But God's guidance is seldom a straight line. We need to learn a lesson here first or accomplish a ministry there next before we reach the final destination.

It's a mystery how the Holy Spirit prepares hearts, makes fields white unto harvest, and puts up roadblocks. We really don't know how divine providence works. But two principles are fairly certain. First, we need to bloom where we're planted. Rattling doors to self-promote or looking for an easy way out is not God's way. We must show ourselves faithful in little things before He will call us to bigger things (Matthew 25:21). God opens and closes doors.

Second, God can guide only a moving ship. The most dangerous condition for a ship at sea is to lose power. The Holy Spirit is like the rudder, which is useless when the ship isn't moving.

My response to God is:

_____

_____

_____

_____

_____

FLEECES

Then Gideon said to God, "If you will save Israel by my hand, as you have said, behold, I am laying a fleece of wool on the threshing floor. If there is dew on the fleece alone, and it is dry on all the ground, then I shall know that you will save Israel by my hand, as you have said."

JUDGES 6:36-37

God did as Gideon requested, but Gideon wanted to be doubly sure, so he requested that God do the opposite the next night (the fleece dry and the ground wet). That is not the stuff heroes are made of, but God answered that request and then reduced Gideon's army to three hundred men, which wasn't nearly enough manpower to defeat the Midianites.

God wanted to show that He, not man, is the deliverer. God chose an insecure man and reduced his army to nothing so the victory would clearly be His. The fleece wasn't a means of demonstrating faith; it was just the opposite. And it certainly wasn't a means to determine God's will. He had already told Gideon what to do. Gideon was questioning His will, just as we do when we ask for a fleece when God has already shown us His will.

Rather than relying on circumstances to guide us, we should pray about every decision, check to see if it's consistent with God's Word, act responsibly, and then with the peaceful assurance of His presence, step out in faith.

My response to God is:

_____

_____

_____

_____

_____

PROVIDENCE

We know that for those who love God all things work together
for good, for those who are called according to his purpose.

ROMANS 8:28

The providence of God refers to God's direction and care over all creation. "He upholds the universe by the word of his power" (Hebrews 1:3), but how God does that is a mystery. The Bible affirms divine providence but teaches no theory of the matter.

The Bible portrays the mystery of divine providence through narrative events such as the story of Joseph. His brothers threw him in a well, but then they brought him up to be sold to a caravan on its way to Egypt. Joseph was promoted from slavery to a high position only to be thrown into prison, and then he was brought before the king to interpret his dreams, which led him to be reunited with his brothers. He said to them, "It was not you who sent me here, but God" (Genesis 45:8).

By "chance" we meet a friend who just happens to have the information we need. With a little "luck" we find the right job. It was a fortunate "coincidence" that led to this venture. But with God there is no luck or any coincidences. Nothing will ever happen to us apart from God's providential care. What happens might include hardship, but He allows that in view of eternity. "This light momentary affliction is preparing for us an eternal weight of glory beyond all comparison" (2 Corinthians 4:17).

My response to God is:

_____

_____

_____

_____

TWELVE BASKETS FULL

The disciples came to him and said... "Send them away to go into the surrounding countryside and villages and buy themselves something to eat." But He answered them, "You give them something to eat."

MARK 6:35-37

The disciples were sensitive to the people's needs, but the Lord said *they* should feed the five thousand. All they had was five loaves and two fishes, but little is much when God is in it. Jesus took what they had and multiplied it until all the people were fed, and the disciples gathered up the broken pieces, which filled 12 baskets.

What an object lesson! But did the disciples get it? They got into a boat to cross the sea, and Jesus went up on the mountain to pray. The Lord saw them struggling against the wind, and "he came to them, walking on the sea. He meant to pass by them" (Mark 6:48). Jesus intends to pass by the self-sufficient. If we want to row against the storms of life, He will let us until our arms fall off. But when Jesus got into the boat, the wind ceased, and "they were utterly astounded, for they did not understand about the loaves, but their hearts were hardened" (verses 51-52).

There is no way the boat is going to sink if Jesus is in it, and He will get us to the other side of a stormy sea. We just have to make sure that Jesus is in the boat with us, because we can't do God's work apart from Him.

My response to God is:

_____

_____

_____

_____

_____

DON'T YOU KNOW?

What shall we say then? Are we to continue in sin that grace may abound? By no means! How can we who died to sin still live in it?

ROMANS 6:1-2

Wouldn't it make the pardoning of our sins even more magnanimous if we continued in our sinful ways? This is an absurd question that obscures the whole gospel. With the pardoning comes new life that frees us from sin, not allowing us to continue in it. We were dead in our trespasses and sin, but now we are alive and free in Christ.

Nobody can consistently behave in a way that is inconsistent with what they believe about themselves. So Paul asks, "Do you not know that all of us who have been baptized into Christ Jesus were baptized into his death?" (Romans 6:3) (and His burial and resurrection—verses 4-5). When we act contrary to who we are, we should ask ourselves, *Come on, don't you know the truth that set you free? Don't you know that you have been united to Christ in His death, burial, and resurrection? Don't you know that you have been joined to God and committed yourself to follow Him? Don't you know these things? Don't you know who you are?*

We should regularly ask ourselves such questions and then reply with conviction, *Yes, I do know who I am—a new creation in Christ. And by the grace of God, I shall live accordingly.*

My response to God is:

_____

_____

_____

_____

_____

THE OLD SELF IS DEAD

If we have been united with him in a death like his, we shall certainly be united with him in a resurrection like his. We know that our old self was crucified with him in order that the body of sin might be brought to nothing, so that we would no longer be enslaved to sin.

ROMANS 6:5-6

God foreknew that many believers would see the cross but overlook the resurrection because it was easier to believe that their sins had been forgiven than to believe that their old self was crucified with Christ. Some try to put the old self to death by "promoting self-made religion and asceticism and severity to the body, but they are of no value in stopping the indulgence of the flesh" (Colossians 2:23). But they can't put the old self to death, because the old self has already been crucified.

Others wrongly reason, *What experience must I have for this to be true?* The only experience that has to happen happened more than two thousand years ago, and the only way we can enter into it is by faith. We cannot do for ourselves what Christ has already done for us. We believe what God says is true and choose to live by faith, and it works out *in our experience*. Trying to make it true *by our experience* will never work. We are saved and sanctified by faith.

My response to God is:

_____

_____

_____

_____

_____

LAW OF SIN AND DEATH

We know that Christ, being raised from the dead, will never die again; death no longer has dominion over him. For the death he died he died to sin, once for all, but the life he lives he lives to God.

ROMANS 6:9-10

Paul's argument in Romans 6:1-10 is based on what Christ has already done for us—that which we could not do for ourselves. His victory over sin and death is our victory because we are united to Him. Paul said, "Know this," not "Do this." Our role is to believe. "There is therefore now no condemnation for those who are in Christ Jesus. For the law of the Spirit of life has set you free in Christ Jesus from the law of sin and death" (Romans 8:1-2). We can't do away with a law, but we can overcome it by a greater law, which is the law of life in Christ Jesus.

To illustrate, we can't fly on our own, because we lack the power to overcome the law of gravity. However, we can fly *in* an airplane, although if we turn off the engine or simply step out of the plane, we will crash and burn. When we are in Christ, the law of death has no dominion over us, and neither does the law of sin as long as we live by faith according to what God says is true in the power of the Holy Spirit. Then we won't carry out the desires of the flesh.

My response to God is:

_____

_____

_____

_____

_____

DEAD TO SIN

You also must consider yourselves dead to
sin and alive to God in Christ Jesus.

ROMANS 6:11

We are to consider true for us what is true of Jesus Christ's relationship with sin and death. This is not made true by experience, nor is it a command to be obeyed. It is a blessed spiritual fact to be believed. Paul now shifts from the past tense (indicative) concerning what Christ has done, to the present tense (imperative), instructing what we must do to live a righteous life. We must consider ourselves dead to sin, he says, but that isn't what makes us dead to sin. We consider it so because it is so. In other words, we are to continuously believe that we are no longer under the dominion of sin.

Death is the ending of a relationship but not the end of existence. Sin is still powerful and appealing, and we can commit an act of sin, not as slaves but as those who are under the dominion of sin. But when it knocks on our door, we don't have to answer. "Sin will have no dominion over you, since you are not under law but under grace" (Romans 6:14).

If we wake up in the morning feeling alive to sin and dead to Christ, and we believe what we feel, we will have a bad day. We will have a better day if we awake and say, *I'm alive in Christ and dead to sin. Thank You, Jesus.*

My response to God is:

_____

_____

_____

_____

_____

THE ENTRAPMENT OF SIN

Let not sin therefore reign in your mortal body, to make you
obey its passions. Do not present your members to sin as
instruments for unrighteousness, but present yourselves to
God as those who have been brought from death to life, and
your members to God as instruments for righteousness.

ROMANS 6:12-13

It's our responsibility to not allow sin to reign in our mortal bodies,
and we do that by not using them as instruments of unrighteousness.
Notice that this passage has one negative and two positive instructions.
Since we belong to God, we can present or dedicate ourselves
only to God, but we can use our bodies as instruments of righteousness or unrighteousness. Our bodies can be used for good or evil. Prostitutes use their bodies for evil, but the good Samaritan used his body
for good (Luke 10).

"We are the temple of the living God...beloved, let us cleanse ourselves from every defilement of body and spirit, bring holiness to completion in the fear of God" (2 Corinthians 6:16; 7:1). You can do that
by asking the Lord to reveal to you every use of your body as an instrument of unrighteousness. (All sexual sins are a defilement of the body.)
When He does, specifically renounce those uses of your body, and then
submit your body to God as a living sacrifice (Romans 12:1).

Finally, submit yourself to God. Resist the devil, and he will flee
from you (James 4:7).

My response to God is:

_____

_____

_____

_____

_____

SEXUAL BONDING

Do you not know that your bodies are members of Christ? Shall
I then take the members of Christ and make them members
of a prostitute? Never! Or do you not know that he who is
joined to a prostitute becomes one body with her? For, as it is
written, "The two will become one flesh." But he who is joined
to the Lord becomes one spirit with him. Flee from sexual
immorality. Every other sin a person commits is outside the body,
but the sexually immoral person sins against his own body.

1 CORINTHIANS 6:15-18

The Creator allows us to share in one act of creation—procreation, which makes sexual sins unique. Sexual unions outside of marriage and God's will can result in spiritual bondage that must be broken. A spiritual and emotional bonding takes place when two become one flesh.

We can free ourselves from sexual bondage by asking God to reveal every sexual use of our bodies as instruments of unrighteousness, including incest and rape. God usually starts with our first sexual experiences and works forward. For each name that comes to our minds, we pray as follows: "Lord Jesus, I renounce [name the sexual experience] with [name], and I ask you to break that sinful bond with [name] spiritually, physically, and emotionally. I submit myself and my body to You as a living sacrifice." Now resist the devil, and he will flee.

My response to God is:

_____

_____

_____

_____

_____

PERSONAL REVIVAL

I appeal to you therefore, brothers, by the mercies of
God, to present your bodies as a living sacrifice, holy and
acceptable to God, which is your spiritual worship.

ROMANS 12:1

Hezekiah modeled the steps for personal revival in 2 Chronicles 29. He began by consecrating the priests (verse 15). Then he commanded the priests to cleanse the temple (verse 16). Hezekiah then ordered the sin offering, which sacrificed only the blood, and the carcass was disposed of outside the city. Finally, Hezekiah ordered the burnt offering (verse 27), which sacrificed the entire body on the altar. When the burnt offering was made, the music began in the temple (verse 28).

Under the New Covenant, believers are the holy priesthood (1 Peter 2:9) and the temple of God. Jesus is the sin offering. He shed His blood on the cross, and His body was entombed outside the city. We become the burnt offering when we offer our bodies as a living sacrifice, which we are urged to do by the mercies of God. Then when we consecrate ourselves and clean out the temple through genuine repentance, the music begins in the temple. We are "filled with the Spirit, addressing one another in psalms and hymns and spiritual songs, singing and making melody to the Lord with all [our hearts], giving thanks always and for everything to God the Father in the name of our Lord Jesus Christ" (Ephesians 5:18-20).

My response to God is:

_____

_____

_____

_____

_____

POWER AND AUTHORITY

He called the twelve together and gave them power and
authority over all demons and to cure diseases, and he sent
them out to proclaim the kingdom of God and to heal.

LUKE 9:1-2

Jesus called the 12 disciples, and they were to follow Him and observe
Him do ministry. The next step in discipleship was to minister
together, and the third step was for them to go out on their own while
Jesus observed. The disciples had seen Jesus cast out demons and heal
diseases, and now it was time for them to do kingdom ministry. They
were to take nothing with them and rely only on their faith in God.

No good manager would delegate responsibility without granting
the authority and power to carry out the task. Authority is the right
to rule, and power is the ability to rule. At that time, only the Twelve
had that authority and power, but it would be extended to all believers under the New Covenant. We have the spiritual authority over the
kingdom of darkness and to do God's will because of our identity and
position in Christ. We have the power to do His will as long as we are
filled with the Holy Spirit. This is His authority and His power, and
therefore they are not operative if we walk by the flesh. "Truly, truly,
I say to you, whoever believes in me will also do the works that I do"
(John 14:12).

My response to God is:

_____

_____

_____

_____

_____

WAKE-UP CALL

Teacher, I beg you to look at my son, for he is my only child. And behold, a spirit seizes him, and he suddenly cries out. It convulses him so that he foams at the mouth, and shatters him, and will hardly leave him. And I begged your disciples to cast it out, but they could not.

LUKE 9:38-40

Sending out the Twelve was a learning experience for them because they had some kingdom-killing attitudes that needed correcting. In answer to the distraught father's request, Jesus said, "O faithless and twisted generation, how long am I to be with you and bear with you? Bring your son here." Then "while he was coming, the demon threw him to the ground and convulsed him. But Jesus rebuked the unclean spirit and healed the boy, and gave him back to his father. And all were astonished at the majesty of God" (Luke 9:41-43).

The two primary qualifications for kingdom work are belief and humility. If we doubt who we are in Christ and the authority we have over the enemy because of our position in Christ, we will likely retreat when the enemy threatens. On the other hand, Paul warned us not to think more highly of ourselves than we ought to think (Romans 12:3). "An argument arose among [the disciples] as to which of them was the greatest" (Luke 9:46), rendering them ineffective.

Relying on ourselves—or rituals, formulas, slogans, programs, or techniques—to set people free doesn't work. Only the truth and Jesus can set us free.

My response to God is:

_____

_____

_____

_____

_____

SATAN'S DEMISE

The seventy-two returned with joy, saying, "Lord, even the demons are subject to us in your name!" And he said to them, "I saw Satan fall like lightning from heaven. Behold, I have given you authority to tread on serpents and scorpions, and over all the power of the enemy, and nothing shall hurt you. Nevertheless, do not rejoice in this, that the spirits are subject to you, but rejoice that your names are written in heaven."

LUKE 10:17-20

This was a crushing blow to Satan's dominion over the whole world. God had given believers authority over demons, and the demons were subject to believers in the name of Jesus. Satan had tried every trick to stop the coming of the Messiah, but Satan made the fatal mistake of orchestrating Jesus's death without counting on His resurrection and ascension to heaven.

The joy the 72 expressed was quickly followed by a rebuke. That demons were subject to them could result in arrogance and pride, so Jesus confronted the first boasting and cut away the root that sprang up in them—the shameful love of glory. For Jesus, however, it was pure joy to see Satan fall, and the 72 to rise above the enemy: "In the same hour he rejoiced in the Holy Spirit and said, 'I thank you, Father, Lord of heaven and earth, that you have hidden these things from the wise and understanding and revealed them to little children'" (Luke 10:21-22).

My response to God is:

_____

_____

_____

_____

_____

THE CONFERRING OF AUTHORITY

Jesus came and said to them, "All authority in heaven and on earth
has been given to me. Go therefore and make disciples of all nations,
baptizing them in the name of the Father and of the Son and of the
Holy Spirit, teaching them to observe all that I have commanded
you. And behold, I am with you always, to the end of the age."

MATTHEW 28:18-20

Authority is *the* issue in spiritual warfare. Two opposing sovereigns cannot rule in the same sphere at the same time. Satan has no spiritual authority over those who are in Christ because God "raised us up with him and seated us with him in the heavenly places in Christ Jesus" (Ephesians 2:6). Jesus is seated at the right hand of the Father, and we are fellow heirs with Him (Romans 8:17).

The right hand of God is the center of authority and power of the whole universe, and the exercising of the power of the throne was committed to the ascended Lord. The elevation of His people with Him to the heavenlies means that they are made sharers of the authority that is His. We have the authority to do His will—nothing more and nothing less. The mandate is to make disciples of all nations, and we do that by making disciples who can reproduce themselves. Like the Twelve and the 72 Jesus sent out, we must be totally dependent on God.

My response to God is:

_____

_____

_____

_____

_____

THE SCOPE OF GOD'S AUTHORITY AND POWER

I pray that the eyes of your heart may be enlightened, so that you will know what is the hope of His calling, what are the riches of the glory of His inheritance in the saints, and what is the surpassing greatness of His power [*dunameos*] toward us who believe. These are in accordance with the working [*energeian*] of the strength [*kratous*] of His might [*ischuos*] which He brought about in Christ, when he raised Him from the dead and seated Him at His right hand in the heavenly places, far above all rule and authority and power and dominion, and every name that is named, not only in this age but also in the one to come. And He put all things in subjection under His feet, and gave Him as head over all things to the church, which is His body, the fullness of Him who fills all in all.

EPHESIANS 1:18-23 NASB

Paul exhausted the Greek vocabulary, using four different words to express the scope of God's power that has been extended to believers. Believers have no instructions to pursue more power, because they can't have more power than they already have in Christ. Therefore, "be strong in the Lord and in the strength of his might" (Ephesians 6:10). His authority is over the entire demonic hierarchy in the spiritual realm but also over human governing authorities on earth, to which we are to be submissive (Romans 13:1-4).

My response to God is:

_____

_____

_____

_____

_____

PERSONAL DEMONS

When an unclean spirit has gone out of a person, it passes through
waterless places seeking rest, and finding none it says, "I will
return to my house from which I came." And when it comes, it
finds the house swept and put in order. Then it goes and brings
seven other spirits more evil than itself, and they enter and dwell
there. And the last state of that person is worse than the first.

LUKE 11:24-26

From the above passage we know that demons can exist outside or inside living objects, preferring swine over nothingness (Mark 5:12). They travel at will and are not subject to the physical barriers of the natural world. They can communicate with each other and speak through willing human subjects like the Gadarene demoniac (Matthew 8).

The use of personal pronouns indicates that each one has a personal identity. The fact that they can leave a subject, come back, remember their former state, and plan reentry reveals they are strategically thinking beings. They can evaluate, make decisions, and combine forces. They vary in degrees of wickedness.

Satan rules this world through a hierarchy of demons, which would be a frightening reality if we didn't know that we have authority over them. The last thing the devil wants us to know is who we are in Christ. So we calmly take our place in Christ, and say, *I'm a child of God. You can't touch me* (1 John 5:18).

My response to God is:

_____

_____

_____

_____

_____

HIGH PRIESTLY PRAYER

I have given them your word, and the world has hated them because
they are not of the world, just as I am not of the world. I do not ask
that you take them out of the world, but that you keep them from
the evil one...Sanctify them in the truth; your word is truth. As
you sent me into the world, so I have sent them into the world.

JOHN 17:14-15,17-18

Jesus was about to return to heaven and leave behind the Eleven. (He had already lost Judas, who was deceived by Satan.) His first concern was that we be kept from the evil one, and the answer is to be sanctified in truth. The church of the living God is the "pillar and buttress of truth" (1 Timothy 3:15). Without the truth, we would never know the love of God. Without the love of God, we would never know the truth.

Jesus said, "I do not ask for these only, but also for those who believe in me through their word, that they may all be one" (John 17:20-21). United we stand, but divided we fall. Finally, Jesus asked "that the love with which you have loved me may be in them, and I in them" (verse 26). The church will be protected and triumphant if we stay committed to the truth, work together in unity, and are known for our love.

My response to God is:

_____

_____

_____

_____

_____

THE ARMOR OF GOD

Put on the whole armor of God, that you may be able to
stand against the schemes of the devil. For we do not wrestle
against flesh and blood, but against the rulers, against the
authorities, against the cosmic powers over this present
darkness, against spiritual forces of evil in the heavenly places.

EPHESIANS 6:11-12

"Let us cast off the works of darkness and put on the armor of light...put on the Lord Jesus Christ, and make no provision for the flesh" (Romans 13:12,14). Putting on the armor of God is putting on the Lord Jesus Christ. We have authority and power over demons, and God has provided all the resources we need. But complete protection requires an active participation on our part: "Take up the whole armor of God, that you may be able to withstand in the evil day, and having done all, to stand firm" (Ephesians 6:13).

We already have on the first three pieces of the armor. "Having fastened on the belt of truth" (verse 14) is our defense against Satan's primary weapon, which is deception. Truth is never the enemy; it's a liberating friend. Facing the truth is the first step in any recovery program. The only thing a Christian ever has to admit to is the truth.

"Having put on the breastplate of righteousness" (verse 14) is our defense against Satan's accusations. The shoes for our feet are the gospel of peace.

Next is the shield of faith.

My response to God is:

_____

_____

_____

_____

_____

THE REST OF THE ARMOR

In all circumstances take up the shield of faith, with which you can extinguish all the flaming darts of the evil one; and take the helmet of salvation, and the sword of the Spirit, which is the word of God.

EPHESIANS 6:16-17

The flaming darts are smoldering lies, burning accusations, and fiery temptations bombarding our minds. Faith grounded in God's Word is our shield, and the size of the shield depends on how well we know God and His Word. Shaky faith is a puny shield. Darts bounce off the shields of mature saints who pay no attention to them.

Every struggling Christian doubts his or her salvation, which is a major reason they're struggling. "But since we are of the day, let us be sober, having put on the breastplate of faith and love, and as a helmet, the hope of salvation" (1 Thessalonians 5:8 NASB). Without this hope, the Christian can easily be wounded in battle.

The sword of the Spirit, which is the word of God, is the only offensive weapon in the armor of God. Paul used *rhema* instead of *logos* in Ephesians 6:17 because he wanted to emphasize the spoken word of God. Satan and his demons are under no obligation to obey our thoughts because they don't perfectly know them.

My response to God is:

_____

_____

_____

_____

_____

TEMPTATION

Let no one say when he is tempted, "I am being tempted by God," for God cannot be tempted with evil, and he himself tempts no one. But each person is tempted when he is lured and enticed by his own desire.

JAMES 1:13-14

God will test our faith, but He can't tempt us for that would be evil. Some question their salvation when they're bombarded by Satan's temptations, but it's not a sin to be tempted. Jesus was "tempted in all things as we are, yet without sin" (Hebrews 4:15 NASB). As long as we're physically alive in this present world, we will be tempted just like Jesus was. But He didn't sin, and we don't have to sin either.

Temptation is an enticement to live independently of God, but Jesus modeled a life dependent on the heavenly Father: "I can do nothing on my own" (John 5:30); "I live because of the Father" (6:57); "I came not of my own accord, but he sent me" (8:42); "Now they know that everything that you have given me is from you" (17:7).

What tempts you might not tempt another, and vice versa. Temptations from without lack power unless a corresponding desire is within. Jesus said, "The ruler of the world is coming, and he has nothing in Me" (14:30 NASB). Identifying the fleshly desires within us is the key to overcoming the temptation to sin.

My response to God is:

_____

_____

_____

_____

_____

CHANNELS OF TEMPTATION

Do not love the world or the things in the world. If anyone loves
the world, the love of the Father is not in him. For all that is in
the world—the desires of the flesh and the desires of the eyes
and pride of life—is not from the Father but is from the world.

1 JOHN 2:15-16

The desires of the flesh" are physical appetites that seek gratification
in this world. "The desires of the eyes" are our self-serving interests.
The "pride of life" relates to self-promotion and exaltation. Satan confronted Eve through those three channels of temptation. "The woman
saw that the tree was good for food, and that it was a delight to the eyes,
and that the tree was to be desired to make one wise" (Genesis 3:6).

Actually, there were no fleshly desires in Eve at the time because
she had not yet sinned, so Satan had to get at her through deception.
He questioned the will of God: "Did God actually say, 'You shall not
eat of any tree in the garden?'" (verse 1). Eve repeated God's command
when she responded, but she added "neither shall you touch it, lest you
die" (verse 3). Then Satan questioned the word of God: "You will not
surely die" (verse 4). Finally, he questioned the worship of God: "You
will be like God" (verse 5).

Those three channels are intended to destroy our dependence on
God, our confidence in God, and our obedience to God. Satan also
confronted Jesus through those three channels of temptation.

My response to God is:

_____

_____

_____

_____

_____

DESIRES OF THE FLESH

Then Jesus was led by the Spirit into the wilderness to be tempted
by the devil. And after fasting forty days and forty nights, he was
hungry. And the tempter came and said to him, "If you are the Son
of God, command these stones to become loaves of bread."

MATTHEW 4:1-3

Satan wasn't pursuing Jesus to tempt Him, because there was nothing in Jesus to tempt (for God cannot be tempted—James 1:13). It was the Holy Spirit who led Jesus into the wilderness to be tempted by the devil. Jesus was alone, isolated, and physically depleted, which aptly describes when we are most vulnerable. Satan wanted Jesus to use His divine attributes independent of His heavenly Father to save Himself. That is what Peter wanted Jesus to do as well, bringing a swift rebuke from Jesus: "Get behind me, Satan! You are a hindrance to me. For you are not setting your mind on the things of God, but on the things of man" (Matthew 16:23).

When Satan wanted him to turn stones into bread, Jesus replied, "Man shall not live by bread alone, but by every word that comes from the mouth of God" (4:4). Jesus quoted Scripture, but what is often overlooked is the fact that He said it. The sword of the Spirit is the spoken word.

Satan has no obligation to obey our thoughts. When tempted late at night and alone in front of the television or computer, submit to God and verbally resist the devil, and he will flee. There is no embarrassment when you are alone.

My response to God is:

_____

_____

_____

_____

LUST OF THE EYES

Then the devil took him to the holy city and set him on the pinnacle of the temple and said to him, "If you are the Son of God, throw yourself down, for it is written, 'He will command his angels concerning you.'"

MATTHEW 4:5-6

Satan deceived Eve by raising doubt about God's word: "Did God actually say…" (Genesis 3:1). He does the same with Jesus by doubting His legitimacy—"If you are the Son of God"—and additionally he tempts Jesus by misusing God's Word. Satan was saying, *In vain God has called You "Son" and has beguiled You by His gift. If this is not so, give us some proof that You are from that power.* But Jesus had no need to prove Himself, and He correctly quoted Scripture: "Again it is written, 'You shall not put the Lord your God to the test'" (verse 7).

God, if you are really there, would you do this one thing for me? We have already given in to the temptation if we begin our prayer with *God, if.* Nor can we cleverly word our prayer so that God must capitulate to our will. He is under no obligation to prove Himself to us. The righteous shall live by faith in the Word of God and not demand that God prove Himself in response to our wishes, no matter how noble they may be. We are the ones being tested, not God.

My response to God is:

_____

_____

_____

_____

_____

THE PRIDE OF LIFE

> Again, the devil took him to a very high mountain and showed
> him all the kingdoms of the world and their glory. And he said to
> him, "All these I will give you, if you will fall down and worship
> me." Then Jesus said to him, "Be gone, Satan! For it is written, 'You
> shall worship the Lord your God and him only shall you serve.'"
>
> **MATTHEW 4:8-10**

The third channel of temptation is to direct our own destiny, to rule our own world, to be our own god. Satan said to Eve, "God knows that in the day you eat from it your eyes will be opened, and you will be like God, knowing good and evil" (Genesis 3:5 NASB). Satan was saying, *God doesn't want You to eat from the tree because He's holding out on You.* Jesus didn't challenge Satan's right to offer Him the kingdoms of the world. Since he was the god of this world, they were his to offer. But Jesus was not about to settle for anything less than the defeat of Satan.

By appealing to the pride of life, Satan intends to steer us away from the worship of God and destroy our obedience to Him. When we manipulate others to get ahead of them; when we lie on our resume; when we compromise our convictions to accomplish a goal; when we smear another to make ourselves look better—beware. That is the pride of life.

My response to God is:

_____

_____

_____

_____

_____

WAY OF ESCAPE

No temptation has overtaken you that is not common to man.
God is faithful, and he will not let you be tempted beyond
your ability, but with the temptation he will also provide
the way of escape, that you may be able to endure it.

1 CORINTHIANS 10:13

Like people who know how to taunt their siblings, Satan knows our flesh patterns. We can't put flesh patterns to death because "those who belong to Christ Jesus *have* crucified the flesh with its passions and desires. If we live by the Spirit, let us also walk by the Spirit" (Galatians 5:24-25, emphasis added).

Temptation will try to get us to go down those old neural pathways in the brain. But instead of finding our own way of escape, we can submit to God the moment we sense the temptation, asking Him to fill us with His Holy Spirit. The way of escape is available the moment we sense the temptation, which begins with a thought. Thinking on a tempting thought will give rise to the old fleshly passions and desires. "Desire when it has conceived gives birth to sin" (James 1:15). We can't stop the birds from flying overhead, but we can stop them from building a nest in our hair. We must remember who we are and choose to think on that which is true. Being unable to do so signifies a lack of genuine repentance and faith in God.

My response to God is:

_____

_____

_____

_____

_____

DEMON-POSSESSED

They came to Jesus and saw the demon-possessed
man, the one who had had a legion [of demons],
sitting there, clothed and in his right mind.

MARK 5:15

Are Christians demon-possessed if they yield to Satan's accusations, temptations, and lies? No, but they are likely defeated, stagnant in their growth, and enslaved to sin. The term "demon-possessed" is translated from one Greek word—*daimonizomai* (verb) or *daimonizomenos* (participle). If it were transliterated as "demonized," it would mean to be under the influence of one or more demons.

The term never occurs in the Epistles, so we have no way of precisely knowing how it would apply in the church age. The problem word for some is *possession*, which doesn't occur in the original language. Possession often implies ownership. In that sense, Christians are Holy Spirit-possessed. We have been bought and purchased by the blood of the Lamb. We belong to God. We are temples of God, indwelt by the Holy Spirit, who will never leave us nor forsake us. Translators were using the word *possession* to mean "Whatever possessed you to do that?" In other words, "What has overcome or influenced you to do that?"

The fact that the man who had been demon-possessed was now in his right mind reveals where the spiritual battle is raged. The severe oppression drove his nervous system to the extreme, giving him unusual physical powers, which would be similar to incredible feats of strength in emergencies like lifting an overturned car.

My response to God is:

_____

_____

_____

_____

HOW DID YOU KNOW?

There was again a division among the Jews because of these
words. Many of them said, "He has a demon, and is insane; why
listen to him?" Others said, "These are not the words of one who is
oppressed by a demon. Can a demon open the eyes of the blind?"

JOHN 10:19-21

After he spoke about His role as Shepherd, the religious leaders
accused Jesus of having a demon (John 7:20). (They accused John
the Baptist of having a demon as well [Luke 7:33]). The Jews were
seeking to kill Jesus (John 7:1), and He asked, "'Why do you seek to
kill me?' The crowd answered, 'You have a demon! Who is seeking to
kill you?'" (verses 19-20). When Jesus revealed what they were thinking, they assumed a demon was giving Him the information. That
would have been a common assumption in that culture because they
had never encountered someone like the Son of God, who knew the
thoughts and intentions of their hearts.

Mediums acting as channels for demons had been around since the
earliest of Hebrew history. One faction in the opening passage equated
"having a demon" with insanity. The other faction correctly pointed out
that a demon cannot open the eyes of the blind. Many present-day psychics believe in Jesus, but not as the Son of God, and they credit him
for having the ultimate of psychic powers.

Without the objective Word of God, we could not accurately assess
the spiritual world that is all around us. We must evaluate spiritual phe-
nomena through the grid of Scripture.

My response to God is:

_____

_____

_____

_____

EXTRASENSORY DECEPTION

When they say to you, "Inquire of the mediums and the necromancers who chirp and mutter," should not a people inquire of their God? Should they inquire of the dead on behalf of the living? To the teaching and to the testimony! If they will not speak according to this word, it is because they have no dawn.

ISAIAH 8:19-20

Extrasensory perception is the awareness of information gained by some other means than natural senses and not deductible from previous experience. Necromancy is an attempt to conjure up the spirits of the dead for purposes of knowing the future or influencing the course of events. Precognition means to know something before it happens.

Imagine the power you would have if you knew about events before they happened. You could be a billionaire just by betting at the race track. To know something before time means connecting with some kind of power that can arrange future events. Satan has limited capacity to do that by manipulating deceived people, but he doesn't have absolute knowledge of the future as God does. Everything Satan does is a counterfeit of Christianity: Clairvoyance is a counterfeit of divine revelation; precognition is a counterfeit of prophecy; telepathy is a counterfeit of prayer; psychokinesis is a counterfeit of God's miracles; and spirit guides counterfeit the Holy Spirit.

Why would someone want to have a spirit guide when they could have the Holy Spirit as their guide?

My response to God is:

_____

_____

_____

_____

_____

DISCERNMENT

Solid food is for the mature, for those who have their powers of discernment trained by constant practice to distinguish good from evil.

HEBREWS 5:14

Solomon said to God, "Give your servant therefore an understanding mind to govern your people, that I may discern between good and evil" (1 Kings 3:9). God did, because his motives were pure. The motive for spiritual discernment is never self-promotion, personal gain, or to secure an advantage over another person. The sole purpose of spiritual discernment is to distinguish good from evil. It's not a function of the mind; it's a function of the spirit.

The Holy Spirit within us won't leave us feeling comfortable in the presence of an evil and oppressive spirit. There is peace in the presence of a compatible spirit, but there's trouble in the presence of evil. We may not know *what* is wrong, but we know *something* is wrong. We need to put that into practice and learn to trust our discernment. It's our first line of defense.

If you sense a check in your spirit, back away. If a pall is hanging over a meeting, stop and pray. Share your discernment with others—"I sense something isn't right"—but don't suggest what's wrong if you don't know. Other believers are likely sensing the same thing. If you don't have peace about a decision being made, share your discernment and pray.

My response to God is:

_____

_____

_____

_____

_____

TREASURES IN HEAVEN

Do not lay up for yourselves treasures on earth, where moth
and rust destroy and where thieves break in and steal, but lay
up for yourselves treasures in heaven, where neither moth
nor rust destroys and where thieves do not break in and steal.
For where your treasure is, there your heart will be also.

MATTHEW 6:19-21

Treasures on earth have two characteristics. First, according to the law of entropy, all systems become increasingly disorderly and eventually decay. Therefore, constant concern is necessary to maintain earthly treasures. Second, there will always be thieves who covet what others have. Therefore, security for our possessions is another concern.

It's hard to be anxiety-free if we're worrying about our possessions (even though we can't take them with us when we die). Storing up treasures in heaven is profitable both for this age and for the age to come. Peaceful existence and a sense of security come from meaningful relationships, not material possessions. Using people to gain possessions reveals what we treasure in our hearts. Peacemakers use their possessions to love people.

"Godliness with contentment is great gain, for we brought nothing into the world, and we cannot take anything out of the world. But if we have food and clothing, with these we will be content" (1 Timothy 6:6-8). If we can't find contentment in ourselves, it's futile to look for it elsewhere. Paul said, "I have learned in whatever situation I am to be content" (Philippians 4:11).

My response to God is:

_____

_____

_____

_____

ANXIETY

No one can serve two masters, for either he will hate the
one and love the other, or he will be devoted to the one
and despise the other. You cannot serve God and money.
Therefore I tell you, do not be anxious about your life.

MATTHEW 6:24-25

People are anxious because they don't know what's going to happen next, but anxiety can reveal a positive sense of caring. If we have an important exam tomorrow, we should feel a little anxious, and the proper response is to study. Anxiety (*merimna* in the Greek) is a combination of *merizo* (divide), and *nous* (mind). James says the man who doubts is a double-minded man "unstable in all his ways" (James 1:8).

The King James Version translation of Matthew 6:25 says "take no thought for your life," emphasizing the mind as the seat of anxious thinking. Jesus asks, "Which of you by being anxious can add a single hour to his span of life?" (verse 27). Anxiety will likely shorten our life span.

Anxiety is a question of trust and single vision. Jesus is saying, *Trust Me. I take care of the birds and the lilies of the field, and you have "more value than they"* (verse 26). So don't worry about tomorrow's needs for food and clothing, because "your heavenly Father knows that you need them all. But seek first the kingdom of God and his righteousness, and all these things will be added to you" (verses 32-33).

My response to God is:

_____

_____

_____

_____

_____

CASTING OUR ANXIETIES ON CHRIST

Humble yourselves, therefore, under the mighty hand of God so
that at the proper time he may exalt you, casting all your anxieties
on him, because he cares for you. Be sober-minded; be watchful.
Your adversary the devil prowls around like a roaring lion.

1 PETER 5:6-8

Casting our anxiety on Christ begins with prayer. "The Lord is at hand; do not be anxious about anything, but in everything by prayer and supplication with thanksgiving let your requests be made known to God" (Philippians 4:5-6). In other words, don't be double-minded about anything. Rather, become single-minded by turning to God in prayer. Then the peace of God "will guard your hearts and your minds in Christ Jesus" (verse 7).

After submitting to God, resist the devil. If believers are paying attention to a deceiving spirit, they are double-minded and therefore anxious. The next step is to state the problem. A problem well stated is half solved. Then divide the facts from the assumptions. People tend to assume the worst. The process of worrying often takes a greater toll on them than the negative consequences they worried about.

Determine what you have the right and the ability to control. You are not responsible for that which you don't have the right and the ability to control. List what you're responsible for and assume that responsibility. Don't cast your responsibility onto Christ. He will throw it back. Any residual anxiety probably exists because you're assuming responsibilities God never intended you to have.

My response to God is:

_____

_____

_____

GOVERNING AUTHORITIES

Let every person be subject to governing authorities. For there is no
authority except for God, and those that exist have been instituted
by God. Therefore whoever resists the authorities resists what
God has appointed, and those who resist will incur judgment.

ROMANS 13:1-2

The early church suffered mightily under Roman authority, and yet the church fathers consistently supported the idea that civil authorities were divinely ordained within their own sphere.

Augustine wrote, "So if anyone thinks that because he is a Christian he does not have to pay taxes or tribute nor show the proper respect to the authorities who take care of these things, he is in very great error. Likewise, if anyone thinks that he ought to submit to the point where he accepts that someone who is superior in temporal affairs should have authority even over his faith, he falls into an even greater error. But the balance which the Lord himself prescribed is to be maintained; *'Render unto Caesar the things which are Caesar's but unto God the things which are God's.'"*[3]

Chrysostom wrote, "Christ did not introduce his laws for the purpose of undermining the state but rather so that it should be better governed."[4]

The church is the conscience of the state, not executor. To rebel against governing authorities is to rebel against God, which makes us spiritually vulnerable to the God of this world. God is saying, *Get in ranks and follow Me.*

My response to God is:

_____

_____

_____

_____

PRAYING FOR THOSE IN AUTHORITY

I urge that supplications, prayers, intercessions, and thanksgivings be
made for all people, for kings and all who are in high positions, that we
may lead a peaceful and quiet life, godly and dignified in every way.

1 TIMOTHY 2:1-2

The temporal authority governmental leaders have in this world is far
less than the authority we have in Christ over the one who deceives
"the whole world" (Revelation 12:9). Being submissive to governing
authorities comes with a promise that it is to our benefit.

Children, you are to obey your parents, "that it may go well with
you and that you may live long in the land" (Ephesians 6:3). Spiritual
leaders and parents should not foster rebellion by speaking critically
about those in authority. Such actions make us an enemy of the state
and serve as a poor model for those who follow us. Rebellious parents
have rebellious children.

Instead, we should respect the rule of law and encourage follow-
ers to pray for us and those in authority over us. "This is good, and it
is pleasing in the sight of God our Savior, who desires all people to be
saved and to come to the knowledge of the truth" (1 Timothy 2:3-4).
"Be subject for the Lord's sake to every human institution...For this is
the will of God, that by doing good you should silence the ignorance
of foolish people" (1 Peter 2:13,15).

My response to God is:

_____

_____

_____

_____

_____

AUTHORITY AND ACCOUNTABILITY

We never came with words of flattery, as you know, nor with a pretext for greed—God is witness. Nor did we seek glory from people, whether from you or from others, though we could have made demands as apostles of Christ. But we were gentle among you, like a nursing mother taking care of her own children.

1 THESSALONIANS 2:5-7

Consider the order of the following words: *authority, accountability, affirmation,* and *acceptance.* When authority figures demand accountability without acceptance and affirmation, they will get only some superficial response. A child is two hours late, and a parent angrily says, "Where were you?"

"Out."

"What were you doing?"

"Nothing."

However, when people know they are accepted and affirmed by authority figures, they will be accountable to them voluntarily. First, the acceptance: "God shows his love for us in that while we were still sinners, Christ died for us" (Romans 5:8). Then the affirmation: "The Spirit himself bears witness with our spirit that we are children of God" (8:16).

Paul could have made demands as an apostle, but he chose to come to them as a nursing mother, as did Jesus. "The crowds were astonished at his teaching, for he was teaching them as one who had authority, and not as their scribes" (Matthew 7:28-29). Jesus had no earthly position of authority; His authority comes with its own authenticity. The onus is likely on the authority figure when children, congregation, and employees won't self-disclose.

My response to God is:

_____

_____

DISCIPLINE VERSUS JUDGMENT

It is for discipline that you have to endure. God is treating
you as sons. For what son is there whom his father does not
discipline? If you are left without discipline, in which all have
participated, then you are illegitimate children and not sons.

HEBREWS 12:7-8

Jesus said, "Judge not, that you be not judged" (Matthew 7:1), but discipline is essential for maturation. God's discipline on His children is proof of His love (Hebrews 12:6). Judgment is related to character, whereas discipline is related to behavior. A father says, "Son, that's not true," and the son responds, "You're judging me." He wasn't judging him; he was correctly confronting sinful behavior. If the father said, "Son, you're a liar," that would be judging him, and he would need to ask his forgiveness.

When our character is attacked, we're tempted to defend ourselves. But that leads to no resolution. All discipline has to be based on observed behavior, and when that behavior is pointed out, the accused can respond appropriately without having to defend their character.

The proper response to confrontation when we've been wrong is to say, "You're right. I did it." We must say we're sorry, and if the sin is toward another, we must ask for their forgiveness. People are deeply wounded when so-called "discipline" is actually character assassination.

Only God can judge righteously. "With the judgment you pronounce you will be judged, and with the measure you use it will be measured to you" (Matthew 7:2).

My response to God is:

_____

_____

_____

_____

DISCIPLINE VERSUS PUNISHMENT

[Fathers] disciplined us for a short time as it seemed best
to them, but [God] disciplines us for our good, that we may
share his holiness. For the moment all discipline seems painful
rather than pleasant, but later it yields the peaceful fruit of
righteousness to those who have been trained by it.

HEBREWS 12:10-11

Fathers, do not provoke your children to anger, but bring them up in the discipline and instruction of the Lord" (Ephesians 6:4). What provokes children to anger is parental judgment and punishment instead of discipline. Punishment is retroactive, whereas discipline is future oriented. We don't punish subordinates to get even; we discipline them so they don't do it again. Spanking toddlers extinguishes bad behavior. God disciplines us so we can share in His holiness. Discipline when properly executed is never painless, but when we respond properly, it yields the peaceful fruit of righteousness. "Whoever loves discipline loves knowledge, but he who hates reproof is stupid" (Proverbs 12:1).

Sometimes the best discipline is to allow the offender to experience the natural consequences of their choices. In all cases, allow God to be the one who brings conviction for the sin. Our job is to confront the sin and, in some cases, determine proper consequences—but not to hammer them home. Many times the best discipline is instruction for better performance. Instruction of the Lord is profitable "for reproof, for correction, and for training in righteousness" (2 Timothy 3:16).

My response to God is:

_____

_____

_____

_____

WHEAT AND WEEDS

The kingdom of heaven may be compared to a man who sowed good seed in his field, but while his men were sleeping, his enemy came and sowed weeds among the wheat and went away.

MATTHEW 13:24-25

Most believers have heard of the parable of the weeds, of the wheat and the weeds (tares or darnel), but even though we're told, few know what the wheat and weeds represent. Jesus said, "The one who sows the good seed is the Son of Man. The field is the world, and the good seed is the sons of the kingdom. The weeds are the sons of the evil one, and the enemy who sowed them is the devil" (Matthew 13:37-39). Wheat and weeds both look like a blade of grass, and they're hard to tell apart until harvest time. "The harvest is the end of the age, and the reapers are angels" (verse 39).

For the church, "wheat" sprouts a head of grain, but the "weeds" bear no fruit. They propagate underground while the church is sleeping. Whenever God sows good seeds in this world who become children of God, the devil sows bad seeds who become children of the evil one. It is unlikely that they are redeemable. We are living in an age when "evil people and imposters will go on from bad to worse, deceiving and being deceived" (2 Timothy 3:13). For example, fake "news" and photo manipulation have become commonplace, so what you see, hear, and read—especially in the mainstream media—can't always be trusted.

My response to God is:

_____

_____

_____

_____

_____

THE TOWER OF BABEL

Behold, they are one people, and they have all one language,
and this is only the beginning of what they will do. And nothing
that they propose to do will now be impossible for them.

GENESIS 11:6

Four essential ingredients make up the success of any Christian ministry: a common purpose, unity among the people, an effective communication system, and a willingness to do the will of God. The descendants of Noah "had one language and the same words" (Genesis 11:1) and were communicating with one another (verse 3). They were united and purposed together to build a tower that reached to heaven (verse 4). With just those three essentials, God saw that nothing would be impossible for them. But what they were doing was in defiance of God. God had commanded them to fill the earth (9:1), not build a city that prevented that from happening. Their desire to make a name for themselves and rebel against God were the same sins of pride and rebellion that caused Lucifer to fall from heaven. All God had to do to thwart their plans was to destroy their ability to communicate with one another.

The first priority of Christian leadership is to discern God's will for their ministry. To fulfill a common purpose, good leaders work to establish consensus among the people through effective communication. Then nothing they purpose to do will be impossible for them.

My response to God is:

_____

_____

_____

_____

_____

TAMING THE TONGUE

Let no corrupting talk come out of your mouths, but only such as is good for building up, as fits the occasion, that it may give grace to those who hear. And do not grieve the Holy Spirit of God, by whom you were sealed for the day of redemption.

EPHESIANS 4:29-30

Half the problems in our churches and homes would disappear overnight if we obeyed the above command. It grieves God when we use our tongues to tear down one another instead of building up one another. James said, "The tongue is set among our members, staining the whole body, setting on fire the entire course of life, and set on fire by hell" (James 3:6). Chrysostom said, "If you let it run wild, it becomes the vehicle of the devil and his angels."[5] James adds, "No human being can tame the tongue" (verse 8), but God can.

"Out of the abundance of the heart the mouth speaks. The good person out of his good treasure brings forth good" (Matthew 12:34-35). A heart fully devoted to God speaks grace to those who hear. "But if you have bitter jealousy and selfish ambition in your hearts, do not boast and be false to truth. This is not the wisdom that comes down from above, but is earthly, unspiritual, demonic" (James 3:14-15). Whether we are a spokesperson for God or a spokesperson for the enemy is determined by choice and the condition of our hearts.

My response to God is:

_____

_____

_____

_____

_____

UNITY IN THE SPIRIT

I therefore, a prisoner for the Lord, urge you to walk in a manner
worthy of the calling to which you have been called, with all humility
and gentleness, with patience, bearing with one another in love,
eager to maintain the unity of the Spirit in the bond of peace.

EPHESIANS 4:1-3

The unity of the Spirit is already present but not very evident. The only basis for unity among believers is to be united together in Christ. Believers are all children of God. Every attempt to unite fallen humanity on any other basis than Christ has failed.

The devil knows what we could accomplish if we were united together, so what is his strategy? First, he seeks to divide our minds because a double-minded person is unstable in all their ways. Second, Satan seeks to divide the family, because a house divided against itself cannot stand. In marriage, two become one in Christ. Third, he seeks to divide the body of Christ because divided we fall but united we stand. "There is one body and one Spirit...one Lord, one faith, one baptism, one God and Father of all, who is over all and through all and in all" (Ephesians 4:4-6).

When believers resolve their personal and spiritual conflicts through genuine repentance and faith in God, there will be unity, and the peripheral things that once divided us will become incidental.

My response to God is:

_____

_____

_____

_____

_____

OVERCOMING PREJUDICES

Put on the new self, which is being renewed in knowledge
after the image of its creator. Here there is not Greek
and Jew, circumcised and uncircumcised, barbarian,
Scythian, slave, free; but Christ is all, and in all.

COLOSSIANS 3:10-11

No racial, religious, cultural, or social barriers exist between those who have been renewed in Christ. In Galatians 3:28, Paul adds, "There is no male and female, for you are all one in Christ Jesus." Imagine a world where there is no sexism, racism, or elitism. That would be heaven, but we can combat the -isms now by working to "present everyone mature in Christ" (Colossians 1:28). Even then, we will still be male and female and have different roles in society, but that doesn't define who we are in Christ. Wives still need to submit to their husbands (3:18) and slaves (employees) still need to submit to their earthly masters (verse 22), but they do so as children of God with equal status in His kingdom. When Paul led Onesimus, a runaway slave, to the Lord, he sent him back to serve his master but "no longer as a slave, but more than a slave, a beloved brother" (Philemon 1:16).

No matter our role, we should "work heartily, as for the Lord and not for men, knowing that from the Lord you will receive the inheritance as your reward. You are serving the Lord Christ" (Colossians 3:23-24).

My response to God is:

_____

_____

_____

_____

_____

NOT MAN-MADE

His divine power has granted to us all things that pertain to life
and godliness, through the knowledge of him who called us to
his own glory and excellence, by which he has granted to us his
precious and very great promises, so that through them you may
become partakers of the divine nature, having escaped from
the corruption that is in the world because of sinful desire.

2 PETER 1:3-4

The Greek word for *divine* occurs twice in the above passage and in
only one other place in Scripture: "Being then the children of God,
we ought not to think that the Divine Nature is like gold or silver or
stone, an image formed by the art and thought of man" (Acts 17:29
NASB). We are not man-made. We didn't even initiate contact with
God; He "called us to his own glory and excellence" (2 Peter 1:3).

Jesus said, "No one can come to me unless the Father who sent me
draws him" (John 6:44). God's divine power is all that we need for spiritual life and godly living, and it's attainable through our knowledge of
Him. In this passage, the Greek word for knowledge means a height-
ened form of knowledge, meaning an intimate "full knowledge"—
knowing our heavenly Father makes us recipients of our inheritance
in Christ and partakers of His divine nature because of our union with
Him. This is not an improvement of our old nature. That was crucified in Christ (Galatians 2:20).

My response to God is:

_____

_____

_____

_____

_____

FAITH LEADS TO UNDERSTANDING

*Make every effort to supplement your faith with virtue, and
virtue with knowledge, and knowledge with self-control...*

2 PETER 1:5-6

Supplementing our faith with virtue and then knowledge would seem to be out of order, but it wasn't so throughout most of church history. The church fathers understood that faith led to understanding. The Enlightenment precipitated a reverse in that order, thinking that understanding would lead to faith. The historical doctrines of the church that failed to meet the standard of human reason were questioned. So it's not surprising that the incarnation, the resurrection, and the Trinity were discarded by liberal philosophers. What they couldn't humanly understand, they didn't believe.

What they really didn't comprehend is that "the foolishness of God is wiser than men" (1 Corinthians 1:25). When we choose to put our faith in God, our eyes are opened and we begin to understand. "Oh, the depth of the riches and wisdom and knowledge of God! How unsearchable are his judgments and how inscrutable his ways!" (Romans 11:33). The finite can never fully understand the infinite. "For as the heavens are higher than the earth, so are my ways higher than your ways and my thoughts than your thoughts" (Isaiah 55:9).

Living a virtuous life may seem to be keeping us from the pleasures of this world, but those who do will understand the value of moral purity and faithfulness later in life.

My response to God is:

_____

_____

_____

_____

SIGNIFICANCE

Make every effort to supplement your faith with virtue, and virtue
with knowledge, and knowledge with self-control, and self-control
with steadfastness, and steadfastness with godliness, and godliness
with brotherly affection, and brotherly affection with love. For if
these qualities are yours and are increasing, they keep you from being
ineffective or unfruitful in the knowledge of our Lord Jesus Christ.

2 PETER 1:5-8

Peter lays out a clear path for significance on which any believer can embark. No spiritual gifts, or talents, or titles, or ecclesiastical positions are mentioned. It's all about becoming the person God created us to be. Godly character is what qualifies us for spiritual leadership. Jesus said, "By this all people will know that you are my disciples, if you have love for one another" (John 13:35). Love is the highest attainment on Peter's list and the goal of our instruction according to Paul (1 Timothy 1:5).

But what if we're searching for significance on another path? Or stagnant in our growth? "Whoever lacks these qualities is so nearsighted that he is blind, having forgotten that he was cleansed from his former sins" (2 Peter 1:9). In other words, we have forgotten that we are children of God. If that is our case, what should we do? "Therefore, brothers, be all the more diligent to confirm your calling and election, for if you practice these qualities you will never fall" (verse 10). What a promise!

My response to God is:

_____

_____

_____

_____

_____

PRINCIPLES OF SUCCESS

Only be strong and very courageous, be careful to do according to all the law that Moses my servant commanded you. Do not turn from it to the right hand or to the left, that you may have good success wherever you go.

JOSHUA 1:7

Joshua's success didn't depend on favorable circumstances in the Promised Land nor on the cooperation of the Philistines. They would be successful and prosperous if they understood and believed God's Word and lived accordingly (Joshua 1:8). We can be successful in the eyes of the world and a complete failure in the eyes of God and vice versa. The first principle of success is to know God and His ways. "Let not the wise man boast in his wisdom, let not the mighty man boast in his might, let not the rich man boast in his riches, but let him who boasts boast in this, that he understands and knows me" (Jeremiah 9:23-24).

The second principle of success is to become the people God created us to be, which is God's will for our lives. Scripture stresses character before career, maturity before ministry, and being before doing.

The third principle of success is to be a good steward of the time, talent, gifts, and treasures God has entrusted to us. "We are his workmanship, created in Christ Jesus for good works" (Ephesians 2:10). Only we can keep us from being successful.

My response to God is:

_____

_____

_____

_____

_____

GENUINE REPENTANCE

When [John the Baptist] saw many of the Pharisees and Sadducees coming to his baptism, he said to them, "You brood of vipers! Who warned you to flee from the wrath to come? Bear fruit in keeping with repentance."

MATTHEW 3:7-8

Suppose a talking dog on the other side of a closed door is saying, "Come on, let me in. You know you want to, and everyone else does. Who would know?" So you let the dog in, and it clamps its jaws on your leg while saying, "You opened the door, you hypocrite. And you call yourself a Christian?" Feeling convicted, you cry out to God, "Lord, I opened the door." That would be confession, but the dog is still there, and the door is still open. You submitted to God, now resist the devil and he will flee. Go back and close the door.

That means get rid of the pornography, throw out the booze, tell your sex partner it's over, stop smoking, pay your taxes, show up for work on time, stop lying, seek forgiveness of those you offended, obey traffic laws, love your neighbor. Repentance isn't genuine without a substantive change in behavior. Paul declared to the Gentiles that "they should repent and turn to God, performing deeds in keeping with their repentance" (Acts 26:20). Repentance isn't complete, however, unless we start living in such a way so as to bear the fruit of righteousness.

My response to God is:

_____

_____

_____

_____

_____

ABIDING IN CHRIST

I am the true vine, and my Father is the vinedresser. Every branch in me that does not bear fruit he takes away, and every branch that does bear fruit he prunes, that it may bear more fruit.

JOHN 15:1-2

Fruit is the evidence of life, but the fruit doesn't grow off the vine. The fruit grows off the ends of the branches that are organically connected to the vine. Vineyards are pruned every year so they will bear more fruit. The dead branches are cut off so they won't interfere with the living branches, which are trimmed back. If branches are not trimmed, they will grow like a bush and the leaves will crowd out the fruit. This is not a hacking process. God knows how and when to trim each branch so as not to damage it. If the branch splits, it dies.

That is why we should not play the role of God in another person's life. "He will convict the world concerning sin and righteousness and judgment" (John 16:8). When God convicts someone of sin, they feel remorseful, and with that conviction comes the power to change. When we attempt to convict others of sin, they become defensive, and that bears no fruit.

That doesn't mean we shouldn't correct someone caught in sin or discipline them, but the emphasis should be on correction, not condemnation. Graceful correction brings about "the peaceful fruit of righteousness" (Hebrews 12:11).

My response to God is:

_____

_____

_____

_____

_____

BEARING FRUIT

Abide in me, and I in you. As the branch cannot bear fruit by
itself, unless it abides in the vine, neither can you, unless you
abide in me. I am the vine; you are the branches. Whoever
abides in me and I in him, he it is that bears much fruit, for apart
from me you can do nothing...By this my Father is glorified,
that you bear much fruit and so prove to be my disciples.

JOHN 15:4-5,8

The pressure is on us! We have to bear fruit, right? No, we don't! We
have to abide in Christ, because if we abide in Christ, then we will
bear fruit. The fruit is just the evidence that we are abiding in Christ.
Apart from Christ we can do nothing of eternal significance. The work
we accomplish independently of God is wood, hay, and straw, which
will burn up when tested by fire in the final judgment (1 Corinthians
3:11 and following).

Jesus said, "By this all people will know that you are my disciples,
if you have love for one another" (John 13:35), which might appear to
be even more pressure to perform. Now we have to do our best to love
one another. No, we don't! Loving one another is the evidence that we
have become disciples of Christ. The life of Christ flows through those
disciples who abide in Him. We glorify God by manifesting His presence in our lives.

My response to God is:

_____

_____

_____

_____

_____

UNABLE TO GROW

And I, brethren, could not speak to you as to spiritual men, but as to men of the flesh, as to infants in Christ. I gave you milk to drink, not solid food; for you were not yet able to receive it. Indeed, even now you are not yet able, for you are still fleshly. For since there is jealousy and strife among you, are you not fleshly, and are you not walking like mere men?

1 CORINTHIANS 3:1-3 NASB

Every believer is alive and free in Christ, but how many are living that way—and why not? Paul indicates that many are not even able to receive solid food. What is being taught in churches is going right over people's heads because of the unresolved conflicts among them. How can we grow if we're prideful and God is opposed to the proud? How can we grow if we refuse to forgive others and God Himself will turn us over to the tormentors?

We should be able to say, *I am more loving, kind, gentle, and patient than I was a year ago.* If we can't say that, we're not growing. Some who are unable to receive solid food are not necessarily unwilling; many are coming to churches hoping to find an answer to their struggles. Spiritually alive churches provide the opportunity for their people to resolve their personal and spiritual conflicts through genuine repentance and faith in God.

My response to God is:

_____

_____

_____

_____

_____

THE PERIL OF CHANGE

No one tears a piece from a new garment and puts it on an old garment. If he does, he will tear the new, and the piece from the new will not match the old. And no one puts new wine into old wineskins. If he does, the new wine will burst the skins and it will be spilled, and the skins will be destroyed. But new wine must be put into fresh wineskins. And no one after drinking old wine desires new, for he says, "The old is good."

LUKE 5:36-39

Form always follows function, but people tend to fixate on the form and perpetuate it even when it's no longer relevant to the ever-changing culture. The metaphors the Lord used don't represent the substance of our faith. The garment and the wineskin are the external dress, and the container is how the substance of our faith is packaged. But time-honored faith and long-established practices become blended in people's minds.

When suggestions are made to change Christian practices, people resist because they think someone is fooling around with their faith. They say, "The old is good," and it probably was good for them 40 years ago. But times have changed, and traditions can become so entrenched that current generations have no idea what function they represent.

The more we're rooted in Christ, who never changes, the less we're concerned about the form of religious practices.

My response to God is:

_____

_____

_____

_____

ROOTED IN CHRIST

Therefore, as you received Christ Jesus the Lord, so walk in him, rooted and built up in him and established in the faith, just as you were taught, abounding in thanksgiving...For in him the whole fullness of deity dwells bodily, and you have been filled in him, who is the head of all rule and authority.

COLOSSIANS 2:6-7,9-10

For Paul, everything centers on who we are in Christ, who is fully God and the head of all rule and authority. We receive Him, become firmly rooted in Him, are built up in Him, walk in Him, and abound in thankfulness for our salvation. The path to maturity couldn't be clearer, but there is a potential fly in the ointment, which Paul identifies in a parenthetical insertion. "See to it that no one takes you captive by philosophy and empty deceit, according to human tradition, according to the elemental spirits of the world, and not according to Christ" (Colossians 2:8).

Paul isn't speaking against philosophy in general, which is the study of nature and the meaning of existence. He's talking about a godless philosophy that comes from human tradition and evil spirits. We can be taken captive if we aren't established in the faith. Paul said, "I am afraid that as the serpent deceived Eve by his cunning, your thoughts will be led astray from a sincere and pure devotion to Christ" (2 Corinthians 11:3).

My response to God is:

_____

_____

_____

_____

_____

SIGNS AND WONDERS

If anyone says to you, "Look, here is the Christ!" or "There he is!" do not
believe it. For false christs and false prophets will arise and perform
great signs and wonders, so as to lead astray, if possible, even the elect.

MATTHEW 24:23-25

God also bore witness by signs and wonders and various miracles and by gifts of the Holy Spirit distributed according to his will" (Hebrews 2:4). Signs and wonders accompanied the apostles in the early church but seemed to diminish in frequency as the church matured, which is evident in the book of Acts. Their purpose was to show mercy to the sick and afflicted, but also to authenticate their message. So it should not surprise us that Satan would, by the same means, attempt to lend credibility to his messengers as the end draws near.

Every occurrence of the words *signs* and *wonders* in the New Testament, either each by itself or in conjunction with the other, is associated with a false messiah, a false prophet, and a false teacher when the context is referring to the end times. That certainly doesn't mean that God isn't working miracles today. Every aspect of our life in Christ is a miracle. But we dare not be arrogant and think that we couldn't be led astray.

The best way to detect the counterfeit is to know the real Messiah, who was sinless and did nothing for personal gain, social enhancement, or materialistic wealth.

My response to God is:

_____

_____

_____

_____

_____

THE COMING APOSTASY

Concerning the coming of our Lord Jesus Christ and our being gathered together to him, we ask you, brothers, not to be quickly shaken in mind or alarmed, either by a spirit or a spoken word, or letter seeming to be from us, to the effect that the day of the Lord has come. Let no one deceive you in any way. For that day will not come, unless the rebellion [apostasy] comes first, and the man of lawlessness is revealed, the son of destruction.

2 THESSALONIANS 2:1-3

Someday the church will see "the Son of Man coming in clouds with great power and glory" (Mark 13:26), but not until a full-scale rebellion against God takes place and "the man of lawlessness is revealed." "The coming of the lawless one is by the activity of Satan with all power and false signs and wonders" (2 Thessalonians 2:9). "For the mystery of lawlessness is already at work. Only he who now restrains it will do so until he is out of the way" (verse 7).

The Thessalonians were alarmed that the Day of the Lord had already happened. From that day to the present, Satan has sought to confuse believers about the second coming—and for good reason. When there are no longer any restraints, "the lawless one will be revealed, whom the Lord Jesus will kill with the breath of his mouth and bring to nothing by the appearance of his coming" (verse 8).

My response to God is:

_____

_____

_____

_____

_____

LAWLESSNESS

Not everyone who says to me, "Lord, Lord," will enter the kingdom of heaven, but the one who does the will of my Father who is in heaven. On that day many will say to me, "Lord, Lord, did we not prophesy in your name, and cast out demons in your name, and do many mighty works in your name?" And then will I declare to them, "I never knew you; depart from me, you workers of lawlessness."

MATTHEW 7:21-23

Prior to the above passage, Jesus said, "Beware of false prophets, who come to you in sheep's clothing but inwardly are ravenous wolves. You will recognize them by their fruits" (Matthew 7:15-16). Then He talks about some who appear to be bearing fruit, but says of them, "I never knew you."

False prophets speak falsely, and demons cooperate with them, but they are puppets of Satan and not doing the will of God. "Such men are false apostles, deceitful workmen, disguising themselves as apostles of Christ. And no wonder, for even Satan disguises himself as an angel of light. So it is no surprise if his servants, also, disguise themselves as servants of righteousness. Their end will correspond to their deeds" (2 Corinthians 11:13-15).

Until the lawless nature of false prophets is exposed, we have to be spiritually discerning. True believers do the will of God and exhibit the fruit of righteousness, which the evil one will try to imitate but cannot duplicate.

My response to God is:

_____

_____

_____

_____

_____

THE GIFT OF PROPHECY

So now faith, hope, and love abide, these three; but the
greatest of these is love...Pursue love, and earnestly desire
the spiritual gifts, especially that you may prophesy.

1 CORINTHIANS 13:13; 14:1

Perspective is the value of distance, so it pays to step back and see the bigger picture to understand spiritual gifts. God sovereignly gives spiritual gifts as a divine enablement for the building up of the body of Christ. Gifts are not an end in themselves, and they come and go. But what remains is faith, hope, and love.

Prophecy is a Holy Spirit-inspired word from God communicated through righteous believers to accomplish His purposes. Prophecy literally means "to tell forth." It can mean to tell *before time* or *before people*. The Jewish arrangement of the Old Testament didn't include Daniel among the prophets because Daniel didn't preach, even though the book of Daniel included many end-time prophecies.

The purpose of prophecy is twofold. First, it is evangelistic, calling people to repentance, disclosing the secrets of their hearts, and causing them to fall on their faces and worship God (1 Corinthians 14:25). Second, "the one who prophesies speaks to people for their upbuilding and encouragement and consolation" (14:3), "so that all may learn and all be encouraged" (14:31).

Any prophetic message not directly from Scripture must at least be consistent with it, or it is not from God.

My response to God is:

_____

_____

_____

_____

_____

TRUE PROPHETS

The prophet who presumes to speak a word in my name that I have not commanded him to speak, or who speaks in the name of other gods, that same prophet shall die. And if you say in your heart, "How may we know the word that the LORD has not spoken?"—when a prophet speaks in the name of the LORD, if the word does not come to pass or come true, that is a word that the LORD has not spoken; the prophet has spoken it presumptuously.

DEUTERONOMY 18:20-22

Old Testament prophets were messengers of God. They never spoke presumptuously, and they spoke with authority: "Thus says the Lord." Nobody had to decide what part of the prophecy was right or wrong. If any part of the prophecy was wrong or unfulfilled, the prophet was deemed false and was to die. (Psychics fare better today even though they're wrong far more often than they're right.)

When Jesus asked the woman at the well to call her husband, she said she had none. Jesus told her she had spoken correctly, because she previously had five husbands and the man she was living with wasn't her husband. "Jews have no dealings with Samaritans" (John 4:9), so she wondered how He could know that about her. "The woman said to him, 'Sir, I perceive that you are a prophet'" (verse 19). True prophets are more than right. They care.

My response to God is:

_____

_____

_____

_____

_____

FALSE PROPHETS

If a prophet or a dreamer of dreams arises among you and gives
you a sign or a wonder, and the sign or wonder that he tells you
comes to pass, and if he says, "Let us go after other gods," which
you have not known, "and let us serve them," you shall not listen
to the words of that prophet or that dreamer of dreams. For the
LORD your God is testing you, to know whether you love the
LORD your God with all your heart and with all your soul.

DEUTERONOMY 13:1-3

Nothing was taken more seriously and dealt with more swiftly in the Old Testament than false guidance. Mediums and spiritists were to be stoned to death, and those who consulted them were to be cut off from the rest of the people. The testing of God in this passage harkens back to Deuteronomy 6:4: "Hear, O Israel: The LORD our God is one."

In this passage, signs and wonders were those that drew people away to serve other gods. So serious was this offense that family members were the ones required to kill those who did (13:6-11). If such people were to persuade a city to follow other gods, all the inhabitants of the city were to be put to the sword (verse 12 and following).

This is just as serious under the New Covenant. But killing people is not an option. What we must do is renounce all involvement with any form of false guidance.

My response to God is:

_____

_____

_____

_____

_____

THE SCHEMES OF FALSE PROPHETS

Thus says the LORD of hosts: "Do not listen to the words of the
prophets who prophesy to you, filling you with vain hopes. They
speak visions of their own minds, not from the mouth of the LORD.
They say continually to those who despise the word of the LORD, 'It
shall be well with you'; and to everyone who stubbornly follows
his own heart, they say, 'No disaster shall come upon you.'"

JEREMIAH 23:16-17

If there is immorality among us, no prophetic message is going to pla-
cate us with pious platitudes like "Hang on. I'm coming soon." "If
they had stood in my council, then they would have proclaimed my
words to my people, and they would have turned them from their evil
way, and from the evil of their deeds" (Jeremiah 23:22). Judgment
begins at "the household of God" (1 Peter 4:17). God is against "prophets" who share their dreams that are nothing but lies (Jeremiah 23:25-
26) and those "who steal my words from one another" (verse 30).

The worst are those who leverage people by saying, "declares the
LORD" (verse 31). If true, we would be disobeying God if we didn't pay
attention to them. Tragic marriages have come about when men have
said, "The Lord told me we're to get married." Pulling rank by using
God's name or claiming special insight into His Word is manipulative.
"This is not the wisdom that comes down from above, but is earthly,
unspiritual, demonic" (James 3:15).

My response to God is:

_____

_____

_____

_____

_____

ANGELS

Do not neglect to show hospitality to strangers, for
thereby some have entertained angels unawares.

HEBREWS 13:2

Bless the LORD, O you his angels, you mighty ones who do his word,
obeying the voice of his word!" (Psalm 103:20). Angels are spiritual and majestic in nature and existed before the creation of Adam and Eve. Their purpose is to execute God's will. They can pass from the spiritual realm to the natural realm, unimpeded by natural boundaries (Acts 12:7). According to Jesus, they do not marry and will live forever (Luke 20:35-36).

Demons have no material form and must work through willing or deceived human subjects or animals. Angels appear clothed in human form, but never as women or children, and never as animals, reptiles, or birds. At times they were so well disguised as men that they weren't recognized as angels (Genesis 18:2; 19:1; Joshua 5:3). Occasionally, angels displayed themselves with a heavenly countenance and clothing that revealed the glory of God.

Those who willfully despise authority "do not tremble as they blaspheme the glorious one, whereas angels, though greater in might and power, do not pronounce a blasphemous judgment against them before the Lord" (2 Peter 2:10-11). Such restraint reveals the angel's godly character, which stands in stark contrast to evil spirits. No biblical record shows that an angel ever appeared to wicked people or warned them of any danger.

My response to God is:

_____

_____

_____

_____

THE NATURE OF ANGELS

The angel of the LORD encamps around those
who fear him, and delivers them.

PSALM 34:7

In contrast to demons, angels are called "the holy angels" (Luke 9:26), "the angels of God" (12:8), and "God's angels" (Hebrews 1:6). Jesus spoke of "his angels" (Matthew 16:27) and "angels in heaven" (22:30). Only two angels are mentioned in Scripture by name. Michael the archangel (Jude 9) is called "one of the chief princes" (Daniel 10:13) and is portrayed as the commander of the good angels who defeated and expelled the bad angels [demons] from heaven (Revelation 12:7-8). The other is Gabriel, the chief messenger who announced the births of John the Baptist and Jesus (Luke 1:11-13,19,26-28).

With the use of the definite article, "*the* angel of the Lord" is believed by some to be a pre-incarnate appearance of Christ, which may have been the case for the "man" who wrestled with Jacob (Genesis 32:2-31). "The angel of the Lord" announced the birth of Samson (Judges 13:3-5). From that visitation and others we can conclude that angels can communicate audibly in the same language and through the same medium as humans. They take on a physical form that can be seen by any person present. They may not always be recognized as angelic beings, but they are recognized as men of God (verses 6,16). They can change their form as they depart from our presence (verse 20).

My response to God is:

_____

_____

_____

_____

_____

THE MINISTRY OF ANGELS

*Are they not all ministering spirits sent out to serve for
the sake of those who are to inherit salvation?*

HEBREWS 1:14

Angels are part of the host of heaven, so we have less interaction with them than demons who fell from heaven and are subject to the ruler of this world. Angels are mediators of God's love toward His children. Their mission is always benevolent:

Angels make announcements. They announced the births of Isaac (Genesis 18:9-14), Samson (Judges 13:2-24), John the Baptist (Luke 1:13,30), and Jesus with a chorus of heavenly hosts (2:9). An angel also warned Joseph to flee to Egypt (Matthew 2:13).

Angels guide and instruct. During the exodus, God told the people, "Behold, I send an angel before you to guard you on your way and to bring you to the place that I have prepared" (Exodus 23:20). An angel also gave instructions to Cornelius (Acts 10:3-7).

Angels guard and defend. God's army stood by to defend Elisha and his servant (2 Kings 6:17). An angel prevented Abraham from sacrificing Isaac (Genesis 22:9-12). Jesus could have called 12 legions of angels to protect Him (Matthew 26:53).

Angels minister to our needs. An angel led Peter out of prison (Acts 12:6-10), an angel ministered to Elijah (1 Kings 19:5-7), and angels attended to Jesus after the devil tempted Him (Matthew 4:11).

And angels assist in judgment, as they did in striking down Herod (Acts 12:23).

My response to God is:

_____

_____

_____

_____

RELATIONSHIPS

Do nothing from selfish ambition or conceit, but in humility count others more significant than yourselves. Let each of you look not only to his own interests, but also to the interests of others. Have this mind among yourselves, which is yours in Christ Jesus.

PHILIPPIANS 2:3-5

Ideally, there is no competition between us in the kingdom of God. He has a place and purpose for all His children. All are significant, and every member of the body of Christ willingly gives of their time, talent, and treasure to the glory of God. Everyone accepts themselves for who they are in Christ and how God created them. Everyone assumes responsibility for their own character and willingly loves others by assisting in meeting their needs and helping them reach their potential.

If we all committed ourselves to become like Christ, we would have that mind among us. Unfortunately, not everyone will, but *we* can, and it is not conditional on whether others do. Relationships break down when we attack another person's character, focus on our own needs, or compare ourselves with others. "When they measure themselves by one another and compare themselves with one another, they are without understanding" (2 Corinthians 10:12). We will never be fulfilled trying to be somebody other than ourselves. God accepts us for who we are. "Accept one another, just as Christ also accepted us to the glory of God" (Romans 15:7 NASB).

My response to God is:

_____

_____

_____

_____

_____

DON'T BE DEFENSIVE

To this you have been called, because Christ also suffered for you,
leaving you an example, so that you might follow his steps. He
committed no sin, neither was deceit found in his mouth. When he
was reviled, he did not revile in return; when he suffered, he did not
threaten, but continued entrusting himself to him who judges justly.

1 PETER 2:21-23

When people attack our character, the natural response is to be defensive. But the godly response is to not retaliate in kind. It's not hard to spot the character defects in others, but pointing them out is not our responsibility, and those who do are in the wrong. Trying to defend ourselves against the judgments of others will only inflame the problem. "A soft answer turns away wrath, but a harsh word stirs up anger" (Proverbs 15:1).

Let them have their say, and then ask, "What do you suggest I do?" No one cuts down another from a position of strength. They're reacting according to the flesh, and a fleshly response from us will only make matters worse. "Beloved, never avenge yourselves, but leave it to the wrath of God" (Romans 12:19). Let God convict them of their sin. In all likelihood they are hurting, and if we can refrain from reacting to their cutting remarks, we might have an opportunity to help them. "Do not be overcome by evil, but overcome evil with good" (verse 21).

My response to God is:

_____

_____

_____

_____

_____

THE ORDER OF SCRIPTURE

Do not lie to one another, seeing that you have put off the old
self with its practices and have put on the new self, which is
being renewed in knowledge after the image of its creator.

COLOSSIANS 3:9-10

Each of Paul's Epistles generally follow the pattern of the indicative (something we need to know) before the imperative (something we need to do). The first half establishes us in Christ, and the second half is mostly instruction about living.

Biblically correct instruction can be given about marriage and family and still produce very little fruit if we're not first established in Christ. Telling an unrepentant husband and wife how to behave as spouses is like instructing two people on crutches how to dance.

If we first establish ourselves free in Christ, then we can live as Scripture instructs supernaturally. "Put on then, as God's chosen ones, holy and beloved, compassionate hearts, kindness, humility, meekness, and patience, bearing with one another and...forgiving each other" (Colossians 3:12-13). Following those verses are instructions for family and work, because God primarily works in our lives through committed relationships for two reasons.

First, we can be a phony in public but not manage phoniness so well at home. Family members will see through us. Second, the pressure cooker of home is where we're supposed to learn how to love and forgive one another. Rather than run away, we must stay committed to one another and grow up.

My response to God is:

_____

_____

_____

_____

IRON SHARPENS IRON

A continual dripping on a rainy day and a quarrelsome wife are alike; to restrain her is to restrain the wind or to grasp oil in one's right hand. Iron sharpens iron, and one man sharpens another.

PROVERBS 27:15-17

A lot of friction is generated when "iron sharpens iron," and some of that is because of gender differences. In this passage, oil and wind represent spirit. Generally speaking, women are more spiritually inclined than men for good and evil. They have a stronger presence in churches, but they are also more inclined to visit psychics to have their tea leaves and palms read. Men are naturally stronger for good and evil. Their physical strength is to defend and provide, but it has also been used to dominate and abuse (1 Peter 3:7). Peter instructs both husbands and wives to refrain from abusing their advantages and to use them for the good of the other:

"Wives, be subject to your husbands, so that even if some do not obey the word, they may be won without a word by the conduct of their wives...let your adorning be the hidden person of the heart with the imperishable beauty of a gentle and quiet spirit, which in God's sight is very precious" (verses 1,4). "Husbands, live with your wives in an understanding way, showing honor to the woman as the weaker vessel, since they are heirs with you of the grace of life, so that your prayers may not be hindered" (verse 7).

My response to God is:

_____

_____

_____

_____

_____

SUBMISSION'S DILEMMA

Older men are to be sober-minded, dignified, self-controlled,
sound in faith, in love, and in steadfastness...Older women
likewise are to be reverent in behavior...submissive to their
own husbands, that the word of God may not be reviled.

TITUS 2:2-3,5

Being in a submissive role is like riding in the front passenger seat of a car—the most dangerous location should an accident occur. Passengers can feel secure in that seat only if they believe drivers know where they're going and are obeying traffic laws. However, if drivers don't know where they're going and aren't obeying traffic laws, passengers can feel insecure. Their natural instinct is to say, "Slide over, buster, and let me drive," especially if they intend to obey the law and know where they're going.

Women's "liberation" is often an indication of poor male leadership. Employees and citizens will likewise respond when employers and politicians fail to show proper leadership. Some stage a protest, while others seek employment elsewhere or migrate to another country.

Demanding loyalty and enforcing submission are focusing on the other person's responsibility when leaders should be setting the example by submitting to God. If we can't be submissive to sober-minded, dignified, self-controlled, loving, steadfast leaders who are sound in their faith, then we're being rebellious. If we aren't striving to be that kind of leader, then we're rebelling against God.

My response to God is:

_____

_____

_____

_____

_____

FALSE FREEDOM

They promise them freedom, but they themselves are slaves of
corruption. For whatever overcomes a person, to that he is enslaved.

2 PETER 2:19

Obesity is a national health crisis, as is the opioid epidemic, but alcohol is still the drug that does the most damage. Many alcoholics are also sexually addicted. It could all stop tomorrow if people could just abstain from using and abusing. Secular diet and recovery programs are law-based, and participants identify themselves as addicts, alcoholics, overeaters, codependents, and so on. They encourage participants to work their programs, which includes following a list of do's and don'ts.

But no program can set us free, because programs don't connect us to God. If abstinence were the goal, then Paul would not have said only, "Do not get drunk with wine" (Ephesians 5:18). He would have added, "therefore stop drinking." He gave us the answer when he said to "be filled with the Spirit" (verse 18). Those who are addicted have a negative perception of themselves. They're angry, depressed, anxious, wounded—and most are tired of living a lie. Even if they could abstain, it wouldn't resolve those issues.

Grace-based ministries don't identify participants by their flesh pattern. We are not alcoholics or addicts; we are children of God who resolve their personal and spiritual conflicts through genuine repentance and faith in God. Self-control is a fruit of the Spirit, and if we live by the Spirit, we won't carry out the desires of the flesh (Galatians 5:16-23).

My response to God is:

_____

_____

_____

_____

TRUE FREEDOM

The Lord is the Spirit, and where the Spirit of the Lord is, there is freedom. And we all, with unveiled face, beholding the glory of the Lord, are being transformed into the same image from one degree of glory to another. For this comes from the Lord who is the Spirit.

2 CORINTHIANS 3:17-18

For freedom Christ has set us free; stand firm therefore, and do not submit again to a yoke of slavery" (Galatians 5:1)—by going back under the law (verses 2-6). "Are you so foolish? Having begun by the Spirit, are you now being perfected by the flesh?" (3:3). To experience our freedom, we need the Holy Spirit to guide us through a repentance process that removes the barriers affecting our intimacy with God.

First, we have to renounce any participation with cult and occultic practices and false guidance. Second, we have to identify and confess the ways we've been deceived by the world, by ourselves, and by carnal defense mechanisms. Third, we have to forgive others as Christ has forgiven us.

Fourth, we need to confess rebelling against those in authority over us. Fifth, we need to identify and confess our pride. Sixth, we have to confess all known sin—especially the entrapment of sexual sins. Finally, seventh, we need to renounce the sins of our ancestors.

Overcoming these seven barriers is the purpose for *The Steps to Freedom in Christ* (see "About the Steps to Freedom in Christ" beginning on page 209).

My response to God is:

_____

_____

_____

_____

_____

RENOUNCE

Having this ministry by the mercy of God, we do not lose
heart. But we have renounced disgraceful, underhanded
ways. We refuse to practice cunning or to tamper with God's
word, but by open statement of the truth we would commend
ourselves to everyone's conscience in the sight of God.

2 CORINTHIANS 4:1-2

The early church would have a rite of exorcism before baptism. They literally faced the west and said, "I renounce you, Satan, and all your works and all your ways." Then they faced the east and made their profession of faith in God. Catholic and Orthodox churches still do this, but to a much lesser extent.

To renounce is the first step in repentance. It means to turn *away* from one thing and *toward* something else. *Renounce* literally means "to turn from," to disown what one has previously believed, participated in, or pledged to. "Whoever conceals their sins does not prosper, but the one who confesses and renounces them finds mercy" (Proverbs 28:13 NIV).

To believe the truth but continue believing lies is not complete repentance. If we declare something to be true, then it is just as important to declare the counterfeit as false. "You cannot drink the cup of the Lord and the cup of demons. You cannot partake of the table of the Lord and the table of demons" (1 Corinthians 10:21).

My response to God is:

_____

_____

_____

_____

_____

BEYOND COGNITIVE BEHAVIORAL THERAPY

Repent therefore, and turn back, that your sins may be blotted out,
that times of refreshing may come from the presence of the Lord.

ACTS 3:19-20

Cognitive Behavioral Therapy (CBT) is the most prevalent method of therapy and counseling in the world and in the church. It's based on the premise that people are doing what they're doing and feeling what they're feeling because of what they've chosen to think and believe. Therefore, if we want to change how people act and feel, we need to help them change what they think and believe.

From a Christian perspective, that is repentance, but how we Christians process CBT is completely different. The secular world is trying to improve their old nature so they can live better independently of God. Secular psychology makes sense only if we are all-natural people living in a natural world, but that is simply not true. We crucify the flesh, renounce the lies, and choose the truth that will set us free. Secularists have no awareness of the spiritual battle for people's minds, so they pass it off as a mental illness and prescribe medications. We submit to God, resist the devil, and then he flees from us. They rely on their natural resources; we rely on God and seek to be good stewards of all that God has entrusted to us.

Sadly, natural persons who get temporary relief from secular CBT are still dead in their trespasses and sins.

My response to God is:

_____

_____

_____

_____

174

SCIENCE VERSUS THEOLOGY

God saw everything that he had made, and behold, it was very good.

GENESIS 1:31

Science is humanity's attempt to understand the natural world, which God has created. Theology is an attempt to understand divine revelation, which God has made known to us. A 50-year-old science book would not be accepted today as a text because our understanding of the universe and how it works has changed. If we are maturing in Christ, our theology will also change over the course of our lives. But what will not change are God and His Word.

It may appear that science and theology are at odds with each other, but the limited perspective of the scientist and the theologian are what may be at odds. When the natural order of the universe and divine revelation are rightly understood, there is no contradiction between them because God is the author of both. We should never fear that a scientific breakthrough is going to discredit Christianity; in actuality, it has been just the opposite. Scientists have confirmed that our mitochondrial DNA proves that we all descended from the same woman and our Y-chromosomes prove that we all descended from the same man, and that God created us male and female. Although many don't want to admit it, biological scientists know that our natural life begins at conception. The theory of evolution is still just that, a theory. We need to question ourselves, not God.

My response to God is:

_____

_____

_____

_____

_____

CHECKS AND BALANCES

You may indeed set a king over you whom the LORD your God will choose...The Levitical priests, all the tribe of Levi, shall have no portion or inheritance with Israel...The LORD your God will raise up for you a prophet like me from among you...it is to him you shall listen.

DEUTERONOMY 17:15; 18:1,15

The king represented the executive branch of government and was to rule according to the law approved by the Levitical priests, who represented the judicial branch of government. The king was not to acquire many horses and wives or much silver and gold. King Solomon violated every restriction (1 Kings 10:26 and following) and divided the country. The priests were to interpret the law, and prohibiting them from having any inheritance in the land was to prevent any conflict of interest. Representing the legislative branch were the prophets and the lawmakers, and they were never to speak presumptuously.

The intended balance of power in our government was divinely inspired, but it breaks down when the judiciary makes the laws, the chief executive is morally unfit and uses the office for personal gain, and the legislators fail to represent their people. A perfect system breaks down when staffed by imperfect people, which is why we need checks and balances and to pray for those in authority. Only Jesus was good enough to be prophet, priest, and king.

My response to God is:

_____

_____

_____

_____

PLANTING AND WATERING

What then is Apollos? What is Paul? Servants through whom you believed, as the Lord assigned to each. I planted, Apollos watered, but God gave the growth. So neither he who plants nor he who waters is anything, but only God who gives the growth.

1 CORINTHIANS 3:5-7

A deacon said to his pastor who was gardening, "The Lord sure gave you a beautiful garden." The pastor replied, "You should have seen it when God had it by himself." In the church age, God has chosen to work through His children to accomplish His purposes. If we don't plant and water, nothing grows. "How are they to hear without someone preaching? And how are they to preach unless they are sent?" (Romans 10:14-15).

The one who led us to Christ and the others who helped us grow and ministered to our needs were assigned by God. On the other hand, nothing will grow if we try to plant and water on our own, for apart from Christ we can accomplish nothing. Just as Satan rules the kingdom of darkness through human subjects, God reigned supreme through Jesus, and now he reigns supreme through us.

Jesus said, "Whoever believes in me will also do the works that I do; and greater works than these will he do, because I am going to the Father" (John 14:12). God's works are no longer limited to one individual. We can do greater works because we are greater in number.

My response to God is:

_____

_____

_____

_____

_____

GOD'S SOVEREIGNTY AND HUMAN RESPONSIBILITY

This is the love of God, that we keep his commandments.
And his commandments are not burdensome. For everyone
who has been born of God overcomes the world. And this
is the victory that has overcome the world—our faith.

1 JOHN 5:3-4

In the mind of God, there is a clear division between what He will do and what He has required us to do (see Figure A). We will be frustrated and defeated if we try to do what only God can do. We can be creative but not create. God will not do for us what He has commanded us to do. God will convict us of our sins, but He won't execute church discipline or discipline our children. Carrying out church discipline and disciplining our children is our responsibility, and God won't bail us out if we don't.

Figure A

God's Sovereignty | Human Responsibility

Uninformed believers experience a spiritual attack and ask God to do something about it, but nothing happens. So they question God's love and their salvation. *Why didn't God do something?* He did. He died for our sins, gave us eternal life, disarmed the devil, and gave us authority and power to do His will. He did His part, but it's our responsibility to submit to Him and resist the devil. It's our responsibility to repent and believe the gospel. It's our responsibility to put on the armor of God and take every thought captive to the obedience of Christ.

My response to God is:

_____

_____

_____

_____

WHO IS RESPONSIBLE FOR WHAT?

*Who are you to pass judgment on the servant of another?
It is before his own master that he stands or falls. And he
will be upheld, for the Lord is able to make him stand.*

ROMANS 14:4

Picture a triangle (Figure B) with God at the top and the bottom two corners an encourager and an inquirer. Each side of that triangle represents a relationship. The most important relationship for encouragers is the one between themselves and God. How we relate to those we want to help, however, is important too. It's also the only relationship considered by the world.

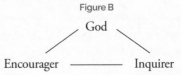

Figure B

Secular counselors learn to show empathy and not be rescuers, enablers, and codependents of the people they're trying to help, which is good but inadequate. The key to successful ministry and healthy relationships is to know who is responsible for what. Playing the role of God in other people's lives will not work, nor can we assume responsibility for the people we love or are trying to help. Everyone has to assume responsibility for their own attitudes and actions. Our ministry is to help inquirers connect with God, and we can't do that without Him. God "gave us the ministry of reconciliation; that is, in Christ God was reconciling the world to himself" (2 Corinthians 5:18-19). "Therefore, we are ambassadors for Christ, God making his appeal through us. We implore you on behalf of Christ, be reconciled to God" (verse 20).

My response to God is:

_____

_____

_____

GOD'S RESPONSIBILITY

The Spirit of the Lord is upon me, because he has anointed me to proclaim good news to the poor. He has sent me to proclaim liberty to the captives and recovering of sight to the blind, to set at liberty those who are oppressed.

LUKE 4:18

God is always present when an encourager is helping an inquirer, and there is a role in both the encourager's and the inquirer's life that only He can fulfill. We can't set a captive free or heal the wounds of the brokenhearted. When Satan has "blinded the minds of the unbelievers" (2 Corinthians 4:4), God is the one who opens their eyes. We can never fully understand inquirers who don't understand themselves, but God knows everything about them, even "the thoughts and intentions of the heart" (Hebrews 4:12).

Jesus, who is the "Wonderful Counselor" (Isaiah 9:6), asked the Father to send us another helper (an advocate or counselor) to be with us forever (John 14:18). The Holy Spirit will guide us into all truth, and that is the truth that will set us free. Although encouragers need to know the truth themselves, the Holy Spirit will teach us all things and bring to remembrance all that Jesus taught (verse 26). He enables encouragers to be wise and discerning. It is not their role to convict inquirers of sin. The Holy Spirit "will convict the world concerning sin and righteousness and judgment" (John 16:8).

My response to God is:

_____

_____

_____

_____

_____

INQUIRER'S RESPONSIBILITY

Is anyone among you suffering? Let him pray. Is anyone
cheerful? Let him sing praise. Is anyone among you sick? Let
him call for the elders of the church, and let them pray over
him, anointing him with oil in the name of the Lord.

JAMES 5:13-14

Initially, the one who is suffering is the one who should be praying. Intercessory prayer is a vital ministry of the church, but it's not meant to replace people's responsibility to pray for themselves. Suppose a younger brother is always asking his older brother to go before their father and ask for things on his behalf. Every good father would say, "Tell your brother to come see me himself." There are no second-hand relationships with God, and every one of His children has the same access to Him. No Christian is to function like a medium, for "there is one mediator between God and men, the man Christ Jesus" (1 Timothy 2:5).

When inquirers ask God whom they need to forgive, God shows them. When they ask God to reveal to their minds every sexual use of their bodies as instruments of unrighteousness, God does. When they ask God to reveal to their minds traumas in their past and the resultant lies they believed, God will. The encourager facilitates that process.

The one who is suffering should also take the initiative to call the elders, and by doing so are assuming responsibility for their own health.

My response to God is:

_____

_____

_____

_____

_____

HEALING CONFESSION

Confess your sins to one another and pray for
one another, that you may be healed.

JAMES 5:16

In this verse, James is referring to being healed from those illnesses that are directly related to sin, which usually fall in the category of what the secular medical profession calls psychosomatic illnesses. A lot more people are sick for psychosomatic reasons than we often realize. "Beloved, I pray that all may go well with you and that you may be in good health, as it goes well with your soul" (3 John 2). If it's not going well with our soul, it's likely we'll have health issues.

According to Paul, not judging ourselves rightly "is why many of you are weak and ill, and some have died" (1 Corinthians 11:30). Bitterness and unmanaged anger can be the basis for high blood pressure and heart attacks. It's a false hope to believe that the prayers of someone else will heal our illnesses if we're eating the wrong foods in excess and we never exercise or get adequate rest. When an encourager helps an inquirer resolve their personal and spiritual conflicts, then "the prayer of a righteous person has great power as it is working" (James 5:16). The Bible tells us that "a joyful heart is good medicine, but a crushed spirit dries up the bones" (Proverbs 17:22).

Other illnesses come from living in a fallen world, natural aging, and unfortunate accidents. For these we need to hold up one another in prayer.

My response to God is:

_____

_____

_____

_____

ENCOURAGER'S RESPONSIBILITY

The Lord's servant must not be quarrelsome but kind to everyone,
able to teach, patiently enduring evil, correcting his opponents with
gentleness. God may perhaps grant them repentance leading to a
knowledge of the truth, and they may come to their senses and escape
from the snare of the devil, after being captured by him to do his will.

2 TIMOTHY 2:24-26

Under the Old Covenant, Satan wasn't disarmed. Only Christ and those He extended it to, which in the Gospels was the Twelve (Luke 9:1) and later 72 others (10:1), had authority over the kingdom of darkness. Under the New Covenant, Satan is disarmed, and every believer has the authority and power to do God's will. The Epistles include no instruction for casting out demons. Under the grace of God, a specially endowed authority agent is no longer required to free people from demonic control.

God works through an encourager who is dependent on Him, one who is not quarrelsome, but is kind, patient, gentle, and able to teach the truth. God is the one who grants repentance leading to a knowledge of the truth that sets an inquirer free. If the inquirer assumes their responsibility to repent and believe the gospel, they will escape the snare of the devil. This is not a power encounter with Satan; it's a truth encounter with God. The encourager helps the inquirer assume their responsibility to submit to God and resist the devil.

My response to God is:

_____

_____

_____

_____

_____

CLEAN HOUSE

Put to death therefore what is earthly in you: sexual
immorality, impurity, passion, evil desire, and covetousness,
which is idolatry. On account of these the wrath of God
is coming. In these you too once walked, when you were
living in them. But now you must put them all away.

COLOSSIANS 3:5-8

Our bodies are like houses that need to be regularly cleaned. We are going to attract a lot of flies if we don't take out the garbage. One person calls the Power Exterminating Service. They study the flight patterns of the flies, try to determine their names and rank, and then cast them out. Those flies find seven other flies and tell them where the garbage is.

A second person calls the Negotiating Exterminating Service. They enter into a dialogue with the flies, trying to extract information from them, seemingly unaware that they're all liars. While they're talking to the flies, the owner blanks out and lets the exterminator assume responsibility for him.

A third person calls the Heavenly House Cleaning Service. They ignore the flies and talk to the owner. Together they clean out all the garbage that has attracted the flies, fill the place with the Holy Spirit, causing the flies to flee, and then they seal off all entry points.

Repentance and faith in God have been the means to resolve personal and spiritual conflicts and will continue to be the answer throughout this church age.

My response to God is:

_____

_____

_____

_____

LORD OF THE FLIES

A disciple is not above his teacher, nor a servant above his master. It is enough for the disciple to be like his teacher, and the servant like his master. If they have called the master of the house Beelzebul, how much more will they malign those of his household?

MATTHEW 10:24-25

Jesus set a demon-oppressed man free, and "the Pharisees said, 'He casts out demons by the prince of demons'" (Matthew 9:34). That is tantamount to accusing Jesus of being a demon. Beelzebul, which means "lord of the flies," is a name for Satan, the prince of demons. Jesus answers His accusers by exposing their logical inconsistency (12:25-27). They were accusing Him of working to expel the one they accused Him of being subject to. That would be a house divided against itself, which cannot stand.

If they malign Jesus as head of the house, how much more will they malign the members of the household? The enemies' strategy is to nullify the message by discrediting the messenger. The more fruit we bear, the more criticism we invite. "Indeed, all who desire to live a godly life in Christ Jesus will be persecuted" (2 Timothy 3:12). But it will all be worth it. Nothing is more fulfilling than to be an instrument in God's hand and to participate with Him in healing wounds and setting captives free. To rescue the perishing, we must weather the storm.

My response to God is:

_____

_____

_____

_____

THE UNPARDONABLE SIN

I tell you, every sin and blasphemy will be forgiven people,
but the blasphemy against the Spirit will not be forgiven.
And whoever speaks a word against the Son of Man will be
forgiven, but whoever speaks against the Holy Spirit will
not be forgiven, either in this age or in the age to come.

MATTHEW 12:31-32

Why can we utter blasphemies against others, including Jesus, and be forgiven, but not against the Holy Spirit? The distinction is made because of the unique works of Jesus and the Holy Spirit. Jesus shed His blood for the forgiveness of sins, and He was resurrected for us to have eternal life. The unique work of the Holy Spirit is to draw us to Christ and to bear witness of the Messiah's work. If we reject that witness, then we never come to Christ to experience salvation.

The only unpardonable sin is the sin of unbelief. True believers who have received the Lord Jesus Christ cannot commit an unpardonable sin, because all their sins are forgiven. The fact that the scribes and the Pharisees saw the evidence of the Lord's power before their eyes and declared it to be satanic is unpardonable. They rejected the witness and refused to believe. Christians can quench and grieve the Spirit, which is unfortunate but not unpardonable. It is a very common strategy of Satan to accuse believers of committing the unpardonable sin and question their salvation.

My response to God is:

_____

_____

_____

_____

_____

PSYCHOLOGICAL OR SPIRITUAL

Since we have these promises, beloved, let us cleanse
ourselves from every defilement of body and spirit,
bringing holiness to completion in the fear of God.

2 CORINTHIANS 7:1

We live in an age of specialization that in practice functions as though the body, soul, and spirit can be treated as separate entities. We fall even shorter of a wholistic answer when we add to the mix the reality of the spiritual world, which is real and more lasting than the book you're reading. "The things that are seen are transient, but the things that are unseen are eternal" (2 Corinthians 4:18). Trying to discern whether a problem is spiritual or psychological presupposes that one doesn't have an effect on the other.

Anyone paying attention to a deceiving spirit has a psychological problem that's going to affect the autonomic nervous system. Jesus was teaching in a synagogue, and "there was a woman who...had had a sickness caused by a spirit" (Luke 13:11 NASB). Jesus said, "Woman, you are freed from your sickness" (verse 12). God relates to us as whole people living in a physical world encompassed by a spiritual realm. We are urged to present our bodies to Him as living sacrifices, to be transformed by the renewing of our minds, and to resist the devil. All are necessary for resolving sexual bondage, chemical addiction, and some psychosomatic illnesses. Complete repentance cleanses us from the defilement of body *and* spirit.

My response to God is:

_____

_____

_____

_____

_____

THE INNER PERSON

Behold, you delight in truth in the inward being, and
you teach me wisdom in the secret heart.

PSALM 51:6

Our inner working is so humanly inscrutable that only God is capable of piercing "the division of soul and of spirit, of joints and of marrow, and discerning the thoughts and intentions of the heart" (Hebrews 4:12). Paul said, "It is a very small thing that I should be judged by you or by any human court. In fact, I do not even judge myself. For I am not aware of anything against myself, but I am not thereby acquitted. It is the Lord who judges me" (1 Corinthians 4:3-4).

When inquirers ask God to reveal to their mind the issues that are holding them back, they are almost always surprised at what surfaces. Many have no idea how deceived, bitter, prideful, rebellious, legalistic, or bound up they are until the Lord surfaces those issues. Although they feel remorseful, they don't feel condemned, because the Lord is granting repentance leading to a knowledge of the truth.

Like Paul, we may not be aware of any unresolved issues in our lives, but that doesn't mean there aren't some. "Therefore do not pronounce judgment before the time, before the Lord comes, who will bring to light the things now hidden in darkness and will disclose the purposes of the heart. Then each one will receive his commendation from God" (verse 5).

My response to God is:

_____

_____

_____

_____

_____

THE EVIL ONE

Forgive us our debts, as we also have forgiven our debtors. And
lead us not into temptation, but deliver us from [the] evil.

MATTHEW 6:12-13

In the Greek, the definite article *the* is before the word *evil*, and many
foreign translations read, "the evil one." The church fathers understood this evil to be the devil. Tertullian wrote, "Christ added that we
should pray not only that our sins be forgiven but also that they be
resisted completely: 'Lead us not into temptation,' that is, do not allow
us to be led by the tempter. God forbid that our Lord should seem to
be the tempter, as if he were not aware of one's faith or were eager to
upset it!"[6]

Chrysostom wrote, "Jesus here calls the devil 'the wicked one,' com-
manding us to wage against him a war that knows no truce. Yet he is
not evil by nature, for evil is not something derived from any nature
as created but is what has been added to nature by choice. The devil is
the prototypically evil one, because of the excess of his evil choices and
because he who in no respect was injured by us wages against us an
implacable war. Thus we do not pray 'deliver us from the wicked ones'
in plural but 'from the wicked one.'"[7]

There is no evil without personhood and choice. Earthquakes aren't
evil unless someone intentionally set off a charge that triggered them.

My response to God is:

_____

_____

_____

_____

_____

SATAN'S SCHEMES

...so that we would not be outwitted by Satan; for we are
not ignorant of his designs [schemes, thoughts].

2 CORINTHIANS 2:11

A weary mother struggling to manage her children has a thought: *Kill your babies.*

A depressed man is standing on a cliff and suddenly thinks, *Jump!*

A boy sits in church, overwhelmed with homosexual thoughts toward the pastor.

Many people are troubled by such thoughts. Many believers even struggle with blasphemous thoughts during church services. But most people won't share those kinds of thoughts with others, and since they can't read other people's minds, they think they're the only ones who have them.

Most mothers and fathers don't kill their children or shoot other people, but they are deeply troubled as to why they would have those thoughts. Some people, however, do kill their babies, commit suicide, or give in to the tempting thought that they're gay when they aren't. Many violent offenders say that voices tormented them until they gave in and committed the crime they were being urged to commit.

Of course, the secular world, or liberal church, calls that mental illness, politicizes the event, and misplaces the blame. Unless we unmask this battle for our minds, many will remain ignorant of Satan's schemes.

My response to God is:

_____

_____

_____

_____

_____

THE INVISIBLE WAR

The Spirit expressly says that in later times some
will depart from the faith by devoting themselves
to deceitful spirits and teachings of demons.

1 TIMOTHY 4:1

What Paul warned about is presently happening around the world. People are having demonic dreams, seeing images in their rooms at night, hearing voices, and struggling with condemning thoughts. Others who are present don't hear or see anything.

For us to hear something in the natural realm, there has to be a source creating sound waves that travel through the medium of air to our eardrums. For us to physically see something, light rays have to be reflecting off a material object to our optic nerves.

What these people are experiencing is a spiritual battle taking place in their minds, "for we do not wrestle against flesh and blood" (Ephesians 6:12). Of course, we can have neurological illnesses, but the content of these dreams, visions, and voices should be a clear indication of the source for those who are enlightened by God's Word.

When children are frightened by something they see in their rooms, uninformed parents look around, see nothing, and tell their children, "There's nothing here. Go back to sleep." If you saw something in your room, would you go back to sleep? Teach them to tell the enemy to leave in Jesus's name, and they will learn that He who is in them is greater than he who is in the world (1 John 4:4).

My response to God is:

_____

_____

_____

_____

_____

GOD'S ETERNAL PURPOSE

To me...this grace was given, to preach to the Gentiles the
unsearchable riches of Christ, and to bring to light for everyone
what is the plan of the mystery hidden for ages in God, who
created all things, so that through the church the manifold
wisdom of God might now be made known to the rulers and
authorities in the heavenly places. This was according to the
eternal purpose that he has realized in Christ Jesus our Lord.

EPHESIANS 3:8-11

The Old Testament made it clear that God would save the Gentiles through Israel, but nowhere are we told that both Jews and Gentiles would form a new creation, the church. This mystery was revealed to Paul, which was difficult for the Jews to accept. Even the angels didn't know this mystery, nor did the demons who suddenly knew that their leader, Satan, was not all wise. Satan knew the Savior would come, and he made efforts to stop Him, but nowhere had it been written that Jews and Gentiles would be united in one body and seated with Christ in the heavenlies completely victorious over Satan.

We, the church, are the present-day stewards of this sacred secret now being made known through us to the rulers and authorities in the heavenly places. All this because of our identity and position in Christ, "in whom we have boldness and access with confidence through our faith in him" (Ephesians 3:12).

My response to God is:

_____

_____

_____

_____

_____

TRAPPED IN SIN

I do not understand my own actions. For I do not do what I
want, but I do the very thing I hate. Now if I do what I do
not want, I agree with the law, that it is good. So now it is no
longer I who do it, but sin that dwells within me. For I know
that nothing good dwells in me, that is, in my flesh.

ROMANS 7:15-18

Paul is describing what it would be like if we allowed sin to reign
in our mortal bodies (Romans 6:12). He agrees with the law, and
he delights in the law of God in his inner being (7:22), which clearly
identifies him as a believer. Something is dwelling in him and operating through the flesh, but it is not him. "I see in my members another
law waging war against the law of my mind and making me captive to
the law of sin that dwells in my members" (verse 23).

The battle is in his mind. Trying to obey the law would be fruitless.
He can't blame the devil, because it was his responsibility to not allow
sin to reign in his body, and now he has to assume his responsibility
to repent and believe the gospel. "Wretched man that I am! Who will
deliver me from this body of death? Thanks be to God through Jesus
Christ our Lord" (verses 24-25).

My response to God is:

_____

_____

_____

_____

CUTTING DISORDERS

I find then the principle that evil is present in
me, the one who wants to do good.

ROMANS 7:21 NASB

One reason some people cut themselves is that they believe there is evil present within them. Some cutters even express the desire to cut out their hearts, which they believe to be evil. Usually they cut themselves where others can't see. They have no idea they're being deceived, so they conclude they're evil.

If people verbally renounce cutting as a means of cleansing themselves, and they trust only in the cleansing work of Christ, they will become aware of the lies they've believed. That alone will not bring total resolution, because something else has set them up to be vulnerable to the father of lies. Many have been abused and suffer in silence (and those with eating disorders become obsessed with appearance in an effort to be loved and accepted).

The origin of the lies cutters believe is the same impetus behind pagan rituals of ceremonial cutting and blood sacrifices. When Elijah challenged the 450 prophets of Baal to call on their gods to bring fire upon their sacrifice, "they cried aloud and cut themselves after their custom with swords and lances, until the blood gushed out upon them" (1 Kings 18:28). Pagans shed their blood for their gods; our God shed His blood for us.

My response to God is:

_____

_____

_____

_____

_____

PRIDE COMES BEFORE A FALL

"Simon, Simon, behold, Satan demanded to have you, that he
might sift you like wheat, but I have prayed for you that your faith
may not fail. And when you have turned again, strengthen your
brothers." Peter said to him, "Lord, I am ready to go with you both
to prison and to death." Jesus said, "I tell you, Peter, the rooster will
not crow this day, until you deny three times that you know me."

LUKE 22:31-34

Satan had fallen from heaven because of his pride. He said in his
heart, "I will ascend to heaven; above the stars of God I will set
my throne on high; I will sit on the mount of assembly in the far
reaches of the north; I will ascend above the heights of the clouds; I
will make myself like the Most High" (Isaiah 14:13-14). Now we know
he is demanding to have Peter, because "a dispute also arose among
[the disciples], as to which of them was to be regarded as the greatest"
(Luke 22:24).

God didn't stop Satan, and even though Peter had the best intentions, he denied knowing Jesus three times. But Peter's faith didn't fail,
and Jesus graciously gave him three opportunities to say to Him, "I
love you" (John 21:15-17), one for every time he'd denied Him.

"'God opposes the proud but gives grace to the humble.' Submit
yourselves therefore to God. Resist the devil, and he will flee from you"
(James 4:6-7).

My response to God is:

_____

_____

_____

_____

_____

THORN IN THE FLESH

To keep me from becoming conceited because of the surpassing greatness of the revelations, a thorn was given me in the flesh, a messenger of Satan to harass me, to keep me from becoming conceited. Three times I pleaded with the Lord about this, that it should leave me. But he said to me, "My grace is sufficient for you, for my power is made perfect in weakness."

2 CORINTHIANS 12:7-9

Protestants have generally understood flesh to mean the physical body in this passage, and therefore they believe the thorn in the flesh Paul mentions is a physical ailment such as poor eyesight. But Augustine, Chrysostom, and the Greek fathers understood flesh to mean our old nature, and they believed that God allowed Satan to harass Paul to keep him from making the same mistake Peter made.

We do know from the text that the thorn in the flesh was "a messenger of Satan," but we really don't know how it was manifested. We also know that Satan's reach is limited and that God can use even him to accomplish His purposes. When King Saul sinned, "a harmful spirit from the LORD tormented him" (1 Samuel 16:14). Paul advised the church at Corinth to deliver a man who had sinned "to Satan for the destruction of the flesh, so that his spirit may be saved" (1 Corinthians 5:5).

We limit the power of God by exalting ourselves, but His power is made perfect through humility, which is confidence properly placed.

My response to God is:

_____

_____

_____

_____

_____

SERVANT LEADERSHIP

You know that the rulers of the Gentiles lord it over them, and
their great ones exercise authority over them. It shall not be so
among you. But whoever would be great among you must be
your servant, and whoever would be first among you must
be your slave, even as the Son of Man came not to be served
but to serve, and to give his life as a ransom for many.

MATTHEW 20:25-28

The mother of the sons of Zebedee asked Jesus to place her two sons
above all others in His kingdom (Matthew 20:20-21), which caused
the other ten disciples to be indignant (verse 24). Rather than climb
over one another to get to the top, we should become as servants or
slaves in the kingdom of God.

Church leaders and husbands, who are heads of the home, are subject to the needs of those they serve. When a special need arises, it's the
responsibility of the elder or the father to either meet that need or delegate the task to someone who can. (Large congregations need a plural-
ity of elders who can organize the people for maximum care.)

Some needs, however, cannot be humanly met, so the greater task
of elders and fathers is to establish their congregations and families
alive and free in Christ so God can meet all their needs "according to
his riches in glory in Christ Jesus" (Philippians 4:19).

My response to God is:

_____

_____

_____

_____

_____

HUMBLE LEADERSHIP

"Eldad and Medad are prophesying in the camp." And Joshua...said,
"My lord Moses, stop them." But Moses said to him, "Are you
jealous for my sake? Would that all the LORD's people were
prophets, that the LORD would put his Spirit on them!"

NUMBERS 11:27-29

The man Moses was very humble, more than any man who was on the face of the earth" (Numbers 12:3 NASB). Imagine what could be accomplished if every leader was as humble as Moses. Successful leaders seek to help every subordinate reach their highest potential, even when it could be higher than their own. It takes humility to rejoice when others receive credit for a job well done, when our contribution isn't mentioned. Who hasn't felt a twinge of jealousy or envy when others are praised for using their gifts and talents?

To be successful, leaders need the contribution of subordinates, because no leader possesses all the gifts needed to build up the body of Christ. God equipped us with gifts and talents, which are to be used to His glory. We should reward those who submit to us with verbal praise and thanksgiving for being good stewards of the gifts and talents God entrusted to them, and we should do so more often than we correct them for the mistakes they make.

Everyone needs affirmation, including leaders whose legacy will be determined by how well the whole body functions.

My response to God is:

_____

_____

_____

_____

_____

HUMBLE INTERCESSION

Moses cried to the LORD, "O God, please heal her—please."

NUMBERS 12:13

Miriam and Aaron opposed the leadership of Moses, claiming equal status, and God staged an intervention. He spoke to all three and questioned why Miriam and Aaron weren't afraid to speak against Moses. When God departed, Miriam was leprous, and Moses prayed for her. Then the whole nation rose up against Moses. God said to him, "I will strike them with the pestilence and disinherit them, and I will make of you a nation greater and mightier than they" (Numbers 14:12).

But Moses was more concerned about God's reputation, and he prayed for mercy (verses 13-19). Finally, 250 chosen leaders rose up against him (16:1 and following), and in each case there was justice. But the sentence was considerably reduced.

If the all subordinates rebelled against leaders, how many of those leaders would feel pleased and vindicated when God brought judgment on the subordinates, especially if God offered the leaders a better venue? How many would ask God to withhold judgment? Which leader would you rather follow? What kind of leader would you like to be? Would you pray for justice or for mercy if your children rebelled?

God said, "I sought for a man among them who should build up the wall and stand in the breach before me for the land, that I should not destroy it, but I found none. Therefore I have poured out my indignation upon them" (Ezekiel 22:30-31).

My response to God is:

_____

_____

_____

_____

ENTRUSTMENT

This is how one should regard us, as servants of Christ
and stewards of the mysteries of God. Moreover, it is
required of stewards that they be found faithful.

1 CORINTHIANS 4:1-2

If God can trust us with money, morals, and message, He will take us a long way. Divine life is not an entitlement where we can demand our fair share. It's an entrustment for which we are to be good stewards, and therein lies the secret to a rewarding life: "It is more blessed to give than to receive" (Acts 20:35).

One of life's great compensations is that we can't sincerely help another person without helping ourselves in the process. Whatever life asks of you, give a little bit more. "Give, and it will be given to you. Good measure, pressed down, shaken together, running over, will be put into your lap. For with the measure you use it will be measured back to you" (Luke 6:37-38). Arrive early for work, and leave a little bit late. Doing just enough to keep the boss off your back may be a fair exchange for salary, but it isn't worthy of promotion.

Two types of people won't amount to much: those who won't do what they're told and those who won't do anything unless they're told. We don't have to be the best; we just have to do our best. Then we look forward to hearing, "Well done, good and faithful servant" (Matthew 25:21).

My response to God is:

_____

_____

_____

_____

_____

LIFESTYLE ILLNESSES

There was a woman who had had a discharge of blood for twelve
years, and who had suffered much under many physicians, and
spent all that she had, and was no better but rather grew worse.

MARK 5:25-26

Nancy is a 50-year-old mother who doesn't eat well or exercise. She's
also stopped going to church. She exhibits many maladaptive psychological and physical symptoms. She's 50 pounds overweight, and
her blood sugar is high. Her doctor overlooks the weight and pre-
scribes an oral diabetes medication. That gives her chronic indigestion,
so she takes an H2 blocker that reduces her digestive symptoms. But
that reduces her stomach acid, which limits the ability to digest food,
reducing her nutritional input.

The medication also puts more stress on her kidneys, and with low
estrogen levels, she gets a urinary tract infection. Antibiotics are prescribed for her infection, which lower her immune system and kill
beneficial bacteria in her colon. The result is a bad case of the flu and
constant gas from a colon imbalance. She starts taking antihistamines
for a sinus infection, and then her doctor recommends a hysterectomy
to solve her urinary tract infection. After surgery, she takes synthetic
hormones that make her feel depressed and weepy, so the doctor pre-
scribes an antidepressant.

Thank God for advances in medicine and competent physicians,
but although they can cure the body, they can't cure the soul. What
Nancy needs is a lifestyle makeover...

My response to God is:

_____

_____

_____

_____

LIFESTYLE HEALTH

I do not run aimlessly; I do not box as one beating the air.
But I discipline my body and keep it under control, lest after
preaching to others I myself should be disqualified.

1 CORINTHIANS 9:26-27

Suppose, instead of seeing a doctor, Nancy confides in a friend she knew at church—someone who has recently been trained as an encourager. After hearing her story, the friend senses that Nancy has some unresolved personal and spiritual conflicts and invites her to attend a small group that's using the *Freedom in Christ* course.

Reluctantly, Nancy goes and meets another friend, who invites her to a YMCA. There she enrolls in an aerobic exercise class. The instructor shares how she has lost several pounds just by eating smarter. They agree to meet and discuss proper nutrition. Nancy finishes the *Freedom in Christ* course, discovers who she is in Christ, and resolves her personal and spiritual conflicts by going through *The Steps to Freedom in Christ*.

After six months of aerobics at the YMCA and eating healthier, Nancy has lost 40 pounds, and her blood sugar is normal. With her personal and health issues resolved, she is less self-absorbed, and she's focusing more on being the wife and mother God has called her to be. Nancy has decided to be trained as an encourager to help others who are struggling through midlife. Freely she has received, and now she wants to freely give to others.

My response to God is:

_____

_____

_____

_____

_____

THE SECOND COMING

The day of the Lord will come like a thief, and then the heavens will pass away with a roar, and the heavenly bodies will be burned up and dissolved, and the earth and the works that are done on it will be exposed.

2 PETER 3:10

You should remember the predictions of the holy prophets and the commandment of the Lord and Savior through your apostles, knowing this first of all, that scoffers will come in the last days with scoffing, following their own sinful desires" (2 Peter 3:2-3). Scoffing and following their sinful desires is the most tragic mistake unbelievers can make about the second coming. Jesus came the first time as Savior, but the second time He's coming to judge the nations. "Do not be deceived: God is not mocked, for whatever one sows, that will he also reap" (Galatians 6:7).

The unfortunate mistake *believers* often make is to see the second coming as the means by which present difficulties are overcome. Failure to assume responsibility for overcoming trials and tribulations and growing in character will also be exposed. We must keep in mind one primary issue about the second coming: "Since all these things are thus to be dissolved, what sort of people ought you to be in lives of holiness and godliness, waiting for and hastening the coming of the day of God" (2 Peter 3:11-12). We should live as though Jesus could come any moment and plan as though He won't in our generation.

My response to God is:

_____

_____

_____

_____

_____

FURTHEST FROM GOD

When all the people saw the thunder and the flashes of
lightning and the sound of the trumpet and the mountain
smoking, the people were afraid and trembled, and they
stood far off and said to Moses, "You speak to us, and we
will listen; but do not let God speak to us, lest we die."

EXODUS 20:18-19

The people of God were encamped at the base of Mount Sinai when "Moses went up to God" (Exodus 19:3). On the third day, the Lord was going to come down on the mountain, but the people were not to go up or they would die. Nobody present that day denied the existence of God.

Two characteristics define those who are furthest from God. First, those who stand "far off" prefer a secondhand relationship with God. They are content to let their pastor or priest study and pray for them. Second, their orientation toward God is to avoid punishment. They live as though the hammer of God could fall on them for the slightest mistake.

But the hammer already fell! It fell on Christ! We are not sinners in the hands of an angry God; we are saints in the hands of a loving God. "Since we have confidence to enter the holy places by the blood of Jesus…let us draw near with a true heart in full assurance of faith, with our hearts sprinkled clean from an evil conscience" (Hebrews 10:19-22).

My response to God is:

_____

_____

_____

_____

_____

SECOND FURTHEST FROM GOD

Then Moses and Aaron, Nadab, and Abihu, and seventy of the elders of Israel went up, and they saw the God of Israel. There was under his feet as it were a pavement of sapphire stone, like the very heaven for clearness. And he did not lay his hand on the chief men of the people of Israel; they beheld God, and ate and drank.

EXODUS 24:9-11

The barrier to the mountain was a test for the Israelites to instill the fear of God to keep them from sinning (Exodus 20:20). The numbers drop off sharply when climbing the mountain of God. These 74 people had an unmistakable encounter with God, but when they were asked to wait until Moses returned, they grew impatient, went back down the mountain, and built a golden calf.

Mountain-top experiences can be exhilarating, but they don't last. We don't build golden calves when we backslide, but we create other gods like appearance, performance, social status, career, family, and temporal gratifications. "Is there a God?" is not the question lukewarm Christians are asking. They're asking, "So what? I believe in God, and I will pay homage to Him, but I have to get on with my [natural] life."

Jesus is our life, and knowing Him defines how we live now and for all eternity. When we love Jesus and others as ourselves, we are living as God originally intended. Godliness is profitable for this age and the age to come.

My response to God is:

_____

_____

_____

_____

_____

SECOND CLOSEST TO GOD

The LORD said to Moses, "Come up to me on the mountain
and wait there, that I may give you the tablets of stone,
with the law and the commandment, which I have written
for their instruction." So Moses rose with his assistant
Joshua, and Moses went up into the mountain of God.

EXODUS 24:12-13

N ow only two are climbing the mountain of God, but why Joshua?
Moses pitched a tent outside the camp and called it "the tent of
meeting" (Exodus 33:7). When Moses went into the tent to meet with
God, the people would stand outside their tents and worship. "When
Moses turned again into camp, his assistant Joshua the son of Nun, a
young man, would not depart from the tent" (24:11). Joshua was like
Elisha, who would not depart when Elijah told him to stay while he
went on.

Some people aren't satisfied fulfilling religious obligations. Instead,
they see what Moses and Elijah had and want it for themselves. They
are like Paul, who said,

> Not that I have already obtained this or am already perfect,
> but I press on to make it my own, because Christ Jesus has
> made me his own. Brothers, I do not consider that I have
> made it my own. But one thing I do: forgetting what lies
> behind and straining forward to what lies ahead, I press on
> toward the goal for the prize of the upward call of God in
> Christ Jesus (Philippians 3:12-14).

My response to God is:

_____

_____

_____

_____

CLOSEST TO GOD

Thus the LORD used to speak to Moses face to
face, as a man speaks to his friend.

EXODUS 33:11

Moses had a unique calling, and he had four qualifiers that made intimacy with God a reality. We can emulate those qualities.

First, Moses was humble, more than others (Numbers 12:3 NASB). Second, he was free from selfish ambition (Exodus 32:9-12), refusing God's offer to make a great nation of him because he was more concerned about God's reputation. Third, his goal in life was to know God and His ways (33:13). Fourth, he desired to see God's glory (verse 18).

In the Gospels, a multitude of people came to hear and be healed, but then they went back home. Of the Twelve, three climbed the mountain and saw the Lord transfigured along with Moses and Elijah. Of the three, "there was reclining on Jesus' bosom one of His disciples, whom Jesus loved" (John 13:23 NASB). Only one stayed with Jesus all the way to the cross. It was to John that Jesus said, "Behold, your mother!" (19:27). The two closest people to God at that time were linked together for the duration of their years.

A vacant place remains on the bosom of Jesus, waiting for anyone who believes that an intimate relationship with God is the ultimate pursuit of life.

My response to God is:

_____

_____

_____

_____

_____

ABOUT THE STEPS TO FREEDOM IN CHRIST

The Steps to Freedom in Christ (Steps) is a repentance process facilitated by a trained encourager, enabled by God's presence, that resolves personal and spiritual conflicts. Several exploratory studies have shown promising results regarding the effectiveness of The Steps to Freedom in Christ. Judith King, a Christian therapist, did several pilot studies in 1996. All three of these studies were performed on participants who attended a Living Free in Christ conference and were led through The Steps to Freedom in Christ during the conference.

The first study involved 30 participants who took a 10-item questionnaire before completing the steps. The questionnaire was re-administered three months after their participation. The questionnaire assessed for levels of depression, anxiety, inner conflict, tormenting thoughts, and addictive behaviors. The second study involved 55 participants who took a 12-item questionnaire before completing the Steps and was then readministered three months later. The third pilot study involved 21 participants who also took a 12-item questionnaire before receiving the Steps and then again three months after. The following table illustrates the percentage of improvement for each category:

	Depression	Anxiety	Inner Conflict	Tormenting Thoughts	Addictive Behavior
Pilot Study 1	64%	58%	63%	82%	52%
Pilot Study 2	47%	44%	51%	58%	43%
Pilot Study 3	52%	47%	48%	57%	39%

The Living Free in Christ conference is now available as a curriculum titled *Freedom in Christ,* "A Small Group Bible Study" (Gospel Light Publications, 2017). It has a leader's guide with all the messages written out, which the leaders can teach themselves; a learner's guide for each participant, which includes The Steps to Freedom in Christ; and a DVD with 12 messages, should the leader prefer to teach the course that way.

Research was also conducted by the Board of the Ministry of Healing based in Tyler, Texas. The study completed in Tyler was in cooperation with a doctoral student at Regent University under the supervision of Dr. Fernando Garzon (currently teaching in the doctoral program in psychology at Liberty University). Most people attending the Freedom in Christ course can work through the repentance process on their own using the Steps. In our experience about 15 percent can't because of difficulties they have experienced. A personal session was offered them with a trained encourager. They were given a pretest before a Step session and a post-test three months later with the following results given in percentage of improvement:

	Oklahoma City, OK	Tyler, TX
Depression	44%	52%
Anxiety	45%	44%
Fear	48%	49%
Anger	36%	55%
Tormenting Thoughts	51%	27%
Negative Habits	48%	43%
Sense of Self-Worth	52%	40%

The Board of the Ministry and Healing is chaired by Dr. George Hurst, who previously directed the University of Texas Health Center at Tyler, Texas. The Oklahoma and Texas data were combined in a manuscript that was accepted by the *Southern Medical Journal* for publication.

Freedom in Christ Ministries
9051 Executive Park Drive, STE 503
Knoxville, TN 37923
(865) 342-4000
Website: www.ficm.org and www.ficminternational.org
Email: info@ficm.org

CAN WE HELP YOU MAKE FRUITFUL DISCIPLES?

The purpose of Freedom in Christ Ministries (FICM) is to equip the church worldwide, enabling them to establish their people, marriages, and ministries alive and free in Christ through genuine repentance and faith in God to His honor and glory. The goal is to make fruitful disciples who can reproduce themselves and make an impact in their community.

We have offices or representatives in over forty countries and some representation in many more: see www.ficminternational.org. Our passion is to help church leaders develop a discipleship strategy that will be effective for years to come. Contact our International Office to learn how we can establish an office in your country or equip an individual representative in your country.

How can we help your church?

We offer:

- Online training for Discipleship Counseling: see www.ficm.org and click on CFN University

- Introductory seminars

- Advice on establishing a discipleship strategy for your church

- Training and equipping for those who will be involved in implementing that strategy

- A discipleship course in many languages to be used in

churches leading participants through a repentance process that establishes them alive and free in Christ

- Many other resources on marriage, depression, fear, anger, etc. (see pages 217-220)

NOTES

1. H. Wheeler Robinson, *The Christian Doctrine of Man* (Edinburgh: T. & T. Clark, 1926), 22.

2. Edwin E. Aldrin, *Return to Earth* (New York: Random House, 1973), quoted in *Current Biographic Yearbook*, 1993.

3. Augustine, quoted in *Ancient Christian Commentary on Scripture: New Testament*, Vol. VI (Romans), Gerald Bray ed., Thomas C. Oden, gen. ed. (Berkshire, England: Routledge, 1999), 325.

4. Chrysostom, quoted in *Ancient Christian Commentary on Scripture: New Testament*, Vol. VI (Romans), 325.

5. Chrysostom, quoted in *Ancient Christian Commentary on Scripture: New Testament*, Vol. XI (James), Gerald Bray ed., Thomas C. Oden, gen. ed. (Downer's Grove, IL, IVP Academic, 2000), 39.

6. Tertullian, quoted in *Ancient Christian Commentary on Scripture: New Testament*, Vol. 1 a, (Matthew 1-13), Manlio Simonetti, ed., Thomas C. Oden, gen. ed. (Berkshire, England: Routledge, 2014), 137.

7. Chrysostom, quoted in *Ancient Christian Commentary on Scripture: New Testament*, Vol. 1a (Matthew 1-13), 137.

FREEDOM IN CHRIST MINISTRIES BOOKS AND RESOURCES

CORE MATERIAL

Victory Over the Darkness has a companion study guide, and DVD, as well as an audiobook edition (Bethany House, 2000). With more than 1,400,000 copies in print, this core book explains who you are in Christ, how to walk by faith in the power of the Holy Spirit, how to be transformed by the renewing of your mind, how to experience emotional freedom, and how to relate to one another in Christ.

The Bondage Breaker has a companion study guide, and audiobook edition (Harvest House Publishers, 2000). With more than 1,400,000 copies in print, this book explains spiritual warfare, what our protection is, ways that we are vulnerable, and how we can live a liberated life in Christ.

Discipleship Counseling (Bethany House, 2003) combines the concepts of discipleship and counseling and teaches the practical integration of theology and psychology, helping Christians resolve their personal and spiritual conflicts through genuine repentance and faith in God.

The Steps to Freedom in Christ and the companion interactive video (Bethany House, 2017) are discipleship counseling tools that help Christians resolve their personal and spiritual conflicts through genuine repentance and faith in God.

Restored (e3 Resources) is an expansion of the *The Steps to Freedom in Christ* with additional explanation and instruction.

Walking in Freedom (Bethany House, 2009) is a 21-day devotional to be used for follow-up after processing *The Steps to Freedom in Christ*.

Freedom in Christ (Bethany House, 2017) is a discipleship course for Sunday school classes and small groups. The course includes a leader's guide, a student guide, and a DVD covering 10 lessons and *The Steps to Freedom in Christ*. This course is designed to enable believers to resolve personal and spiritual conflicts and be established alive and free in Christ.

The Bondage Breaker DVD Experience (Harvest House, 2011) is also a discipleship course for Sunday school classes and small groups. It is similar to the one above, but the lessons are 15 minutes long instead of 30 minutes. It has a companion interactive workbook, but no leader's guide.

"Victory Series" (Bethany House, 2014-2015) is a comprehensive curriculum, including eight books that follow the growth sequence of being rooted in Christ, growing in Christ, living in Christ, and overcoming in Christ: *God's Story for You; Your New Identity; Your Foundation in Christ; Renewing Your Mind; Growing in Christ; Your Life in Christ; Your Authority in Christ; Your Ultimate Victory.*

SPECIALIZED BOOKS

The Bondage Breaker, The Next Step (Harvest House, 2011) includes several testimonies of people who found their freedom from all kinds of problems, with commentary by Dr. Anderson. It is an important learning tool for encouragers and gives hope to those who are entangled in sin.

Overcoming Addictive Behavior with Mike Quarles (Bethany House, 2003) explores the path to addiction and how a Christian can overcome addictive behaviors.

Overcoming Depression with Joanne Anderson (Bethany House, 2004) explores the nature of depression, which is a body, soul, and spirit problem and presents a wholistic answer for overcoming this "common cold" of mental illnesses.

Daily in Christ with Joanne Anderson (Harvest House, 2000) is a popular daily devotional read by thousands of internet subscribers every day.

Who I Am in Christ (Bethany House, 2001) has 36 short chapters describing who believers are in Christ and how their deepest needs are met in Him.

Freedom from Addiction with Mike and Julia Quarles (Bethany House, 1996) begins with Mike and Julia's journey into addiction and codependency, and explains the nature of chemical addictions and how to overcome them in Christ.

One Day at a Time with Mike and Julia Quarles (Bethany House, 2000) is a 120-day devotional helping those who struggle with addictive behaviors and explaining how to discover the grace of God on a daily basis.

Letting Go of Fears with Rich Miller (Harvest House Publishers, 2018) explains the nature of fear, anxiety, and panic attacks and how to overcome them.

Setting Your Church Free with Charles Mylander (Bethany House, 2014) explains servant leadership and how the leadership of a church can resolve corporate conflicts through corporate repentance.

Setting Your Marriage Free with Charles Mylander (Bethany House, 2014) explains God's divine plan for marriage and the steps that couples can take to resolve their difficulties.

Christ-Centered Therapy with Terry and Julianne Zuehlke (Zondervan, 2000) explains the practical integration of theology and psychology for professional counselors, and provides them with biblical tools for therapy.

Managing Your Anger with Rich Miller (Harvest House, 2018) explains the nature of anger and how to put away all anger, wrath, and malice.

Grace That Breaks the Chains with Rich Miller and Paul Travis (Harvest House, 2014) explains the bondage of legalism and how to overcome it by the grace of God.

Winning the Battle Within (Harvest House, 2008) shares God's standards for sexual conduct, the path to sexual addiction, and how to overcome sexual strongholds.

Restoring Broken Relationships (Bethany House, 2015) explains the primary ministry of the church, and how we can be reconciled to God and each other.

Rough Road to Freedom (Monarch Books, 2012) is Dr. Anderson's memoir.

The Power of Presence (Monarch Books, 2016) is about experiencing the presence of God during difficult times and what our presence means to each other. This book is written in the context of Dr. Anderson caring for his wife, who is slowly dying with agitated dementia.

For more information or to purchase the above materials contact
Freedom In Christ Ministries:

Canada:
freedominchrist@sasktel.net
www.ficm.ca

United Kingdom:
info@ficm.org.uk
www.ficm.org.uk

United States:
info@ficm.org
www.ficm.org

International:
www.ficminternational.org

To learn more about Harvest House books and
to read sample chapters, visit our website:

www.harvesthousepublishers.com

HARVEST HOUSE PUBLISHERS
EUGENE, OREGON